Essential ELTON

Essential ELTON

by Spencer Bright

First published in Great Britain in 1998 by Chameleon Books
an imprint of Andre Deutsch Ltd
76 Dean Street
London W1V 5HA

Andre Deutsch Ltd is a subsidiary of VCI plc

10 9 8 7 6 5 4 3 2 1

Printed and bound by Jarrold Book Printing, Thetford, Norfolk

A catalogue record for this book is available from the British Library
ISBN 0 233 99361 4

To the memory of Paul Vaughan-Phillips

Contents

Contents

Skyline Pigeon

Skyline Pigeon

Recorded: Between December 1968 and April 1969, Dick James Studios,
James House, 71-75 New Oxford Street, London
First released: Empty Sky album, June 1969

REG DWIGHT WAS A CHILD PRODIGY who studied piano and sung in the choir at
the Royal Academy of Music in London. He hated being force-fed classical music
and much preferred pop. In 1967, aged 20, he was already a professional
pianist and back-up vocalist with Bluesology, a soul band he had formed with
friends. They played esoteric blues, jazz and soul and backed visiting American
R&B stars, before becoming the backing band of soon-to-be chart-topping British
blues crooner, Long John Baldry.

Bernie Taupin, just turned 17, was a labourer with a rebellious streak. He
liked writing poetry and reading tales of nether worlds and derring-do, particularly about American history and the grit-filled lives of cowboys.

Both had received an invitation from Ray Williams of Liberty Records, to
audition at his office in swanky Albemarle Street, Mayfair, after replying to a
talent-spotting ad in the *New Musical Express*.. For Bernie, the offer to pop in if
he was passing would mean a 150-mile trip from his home on a farm in
Lincolnshire. It was an easier journey for Reg Dwight. He was born and lived in
Northwood Hills on the Middlesex perimeter of London. Northwood was
notable only for housing HMS *Warrior,* an armed services and NATO base, and
was therefore a surefire target for any Soviet Cold War missiles.

Reg sang an old Jim Reeves number at his audition, recalled from his days
playing in pubs and clubs. Williams was not able to offer him a recording deal,
but detecting some talent asked if Reg wrote songs. Yes, he could write tunes
(though he had barely tried), but was not so good at words. Williams, with
Bernie's poems purporting to be lyrics on his desk, handed them to Reg, with the
instruction to have a go.

At home, Reg found it easy to match melodies to the words of Bernie Taupin,
even if they were a bit flower-powery. Soon Reg had written around 20 tunes to
Bernie's lyrics. As well as his work with Bluesology, Reg was writing and
demo-ing songs at the West End studio of Dick James Music, publishers of The

Beatles, among others. Williams also sent Bernie along to the studio. Noticing this unprepossessing boy in the corner, Reg asked if he was the lyricist. The future lifelong partners adjourned for coffee and bonded over their enthusiasm for collecting records and an appreciation for pop, in all its varied glory.

At the time, the Dick James Studio was open to all musicians and associate publishing companies that had business arrangements with Dick James Music (DJM). It was a little too open, however, enabling Elton and Bernie to make 50-odd unauthorised demos in the tiny four-track studio. Although Dick James cleared out many of the musicians who abused the system, he kept Reg and Bernie because he liked their demos. In November 1967, he signed them to a publishing contract, followed by a separate recording contract for Reg two months later.

As a salaried songwriter, Reg could say goodbye to Bluesology, though not before taking a life-long memento. He wanted rid of Reginald Kenneth Dwight, the fusty birth-name he berated his parents for giving him. He was after something with a hint of artiness and a promise of charisma. He looked no further than his colleagues Elton Dean, the saxophone player in Bluesology and later member of the progressive jazz group Soft Machine, and Long John Baldry. For an extra flourish he chose the middle name Hercules, inspired less by the strong man of legend than, as his mother pointed out, the clapped-out carthorse on the TV comedy show, *Steptoe and Son.*

Bernie Taupin and Elton John were following the traditions of Tin Pan Alley, writing songs for other artists to cover. Grateful to be paid to write at all, they penned songs with drearily predictable titles like Turn To Me and When The First Tear Shows, plus some that suggested a glimmer of originality, such as Smokestack Children and The Tide Will Turn For Rebecca.

Their efforts were recorded as demos; some, like Velvet Fountain, a sludgy Lucy In The Sky With Diamonds take-off, still survive. But writing to order was not their strength and they were thrilled when, a year later, I Can't Go On Living Without You made it to the final six British nominations for the 1969 Eurovision Song Contest. Sung on TV by Lulu, no less, this was some kind of recognition, even if they did have misgivings about the song's artistic value.

Elton and Bernie's saviour was new DJM song plugger Steve Brown, who

Skyline Pigeon

thought their material was rubbish. He told the deflated Elton that it didn't make sense to be listening to mainly American West Coast music and writing English bubblegum pop. He suggested they write the music they would like to listen to, rather than trying to second-guess Dick James.

Skyline Pigeon was the first expression of that liberation. Its qualities were recognised by the two DJM artists who quickly covered it. Roger Cook had already been in the charts with the duo David and Jonathan and would become a successful songwriter and member of the group Blue Mink with partner Roger Greenaway; and Guy Darrell received radio airplay for his version of the single. For Elton John and Bernie Taupin, this was breakthrough time.

Elton John's own version, recorded for the Empty Sky sessions, contains the template for all the great work to come. His voice varies from a smooth maturity in the middle register to faltering wobbles as it rises. His keyboard playing is stiffly unyielding though proficient. The song opens with a baroque harpsichord trilling pseudo-Bach, which harks back to Saturday-morning lessons at the Royal Academy. After a few bars, the wistful folky tenor soars and floats over the staccato melody. As the heartfelt voice packs all its yearning into the chorus line of 'Fly away', it speaks of imprisoned souls waiting to be released and the joy of imagined flight. Behind a veneer of precocious professionalism, the delivery shows something of a lack of self-confidence.

Elton, never happy with the original rendition, was to re-record the song three years later, playing piano. It was released on the B-side of Daniel, where it has the benefit of Paul Buckmaster's uncharacteristically muted orchestral arrangement. Though more majestic, it lacks the ingenue quality of the initial recording.

Bernie Taupin thought Skyline Pigeon was the first really good song they had written together. His inspiration for the theme had come from a 12th-century clocktower he often climbed as a child to admire the sunsets. Although never released as an A-side, Elton regarded it as the truly outstanding track on the Empty Sky album.

Lady Samantha

Recorded: December 1968, Dick James Studio, London
First released: coupled with All Across The Heavens, January 1969

BERNIE TAUPIN RETREATED TO LINCOLNSHIRE for the first year after his initial meetings with Reg Dwight, returning from time to time to hang out with Reg at DJM's studio and offices in New Oxford Street. The new friends started to bond closely when they moved in together, first to a flat in Islington, North London and then back with Elton's mother and stepfather in Northwood Hills. It was here that their songwriting rapidly started to mature. Bernie would write the lyrics alone and hand them to Reg at the upright piano in the sitting room, a pattern that has in essence never changed.

They were starting to justify their contract with Dick James Music. Lady Samantha was realised in the first wave of creative freedom encouraged by Steve Brown, who was revolutionising the atmosphere at a company that knew a lot about publishing but little about how to develop new artists.

The first recording by Elton of his and Bernie's work, Lady Samantha, was a recognisable piece of craftsmanship. It was streets ahead of their crude first songwriting effort Scarecrow, and other early tortuously titled gems such as Swan Queen Of The Laughing Lake and A Dandelion Dies In The Wind.

Lady Samantha was recorded at the DJM studio with the in-house band of Caleb Quaye on guitar (a friend since the days when Elton was a tea boy at a music publishers), drummer Roger Pope (who was in Hookfoot with Quaye), and bass player Tony Murray. In an era when it was still possible to try your untrained hand at the art of recording, Steve Brown took on the mantle of producer.

The session was temporarily stalled when Elton discovered that his rented electric piano had an out-of-tune B flat. The tune was written in the key of B flat and Elton needed the note. Fortunately he had the skills to transpose the song so that he could accommodate the piano's idiosyncrasies.

Lady Samantha

There is a whiff of Procul Harum and English psychedelia as the song sways between dreamy verse and pop chorus. It rocks with wailing electric guitar then swings with a swirling organ and choppy riffs behind Elton's boyish voice. Bernie's Lady Samantha is a demented Emily Bronte figure tragically wandering the hillsides lost in her distracted melancholy. At influential BBC Radio 1, DJs at opposite ends of the taste spectrum, from Jimmy Young to John Peel, played Lady Samantha. The public, however, were to remain unimpressed. This was the second attempt by DJM to establish Elton John as an artist. His first single, I've Been Loving You, though credited to Elton and Bernie, was all Elton's work. It was chosen by Dick James, who believed that Elton could be another Engelbert Humperdinck or Tom Jones. The vocal performance on I've Been Loving You was strong but Elton was fighting too big a battle with a sub-standard cabaret tune. Elton included his partner's name on the song because he felt embarrassed that the two songs on the single, including the B-side Here's To The Next Time, were not a result of their own shared sweat.

The press release for I've Been Loving You hailed Elton John as the great new talent of the year and chided, 'You have been warned.' The disc spluttered once or twice over the wheezy signal of Radio Luxembourg, the Continental-based commercial pop station, but the promised new talent of 1968 would have to skip 1969 and wait for 1970 before starting to live up to the hype.

Encouraged by the response to Lady Samantha, a third single, It's Me That You Need, was released in May 1969 on the newly formed DJM label. Lacking any distinction, it too failed to reach pop heights. By now, the album Empty Sky had been completed. Dick James decided to release it although there was no hit single or noticeable following for his protégé. His instincts were paternal and his pockets were deep enough.

Empty Sky was released in June 1969. Despite the mystical overtones of tracks like Val-Hala and Hymn 2000, the cover drawing of a neat singer at his piano wearing a trendy jacket hinted at someone more mainstream.

The album failed to make a dent on the British charts though it made the American charts in 1975 when released in the wake of Elton John's superstardom. Lady Samantha was covered in 1969 by West Coast band Three Dog Night on their album Suitable for Framing. Elton and Bernie watched as it climbed the Billboard chart, proud that they could claim part of the glory. EJ

Border Song

Recorded: January 1970, Trident Studios, St. Anne's Court, London
First released: c/w Bad Side of the Moon, 20 March, 1970

FEW BRITISH WHITE MUSICIANS of any age in the late 1960s can have matched Elton John's experience of playing with a core of formative names in soul music. As piano player for Bluesology, he toured one-nighters with some legendary R&B screamers and growlers, balladeers and show-offs like Major Lance, Solomon Burke, Billy Stewart, Arthur Alexander, Lee Dorsey, The Exciters and Patti LaBelle and The Blue Belles.

Elton was a big fan of black music. His father Stanley introduced him to the less than raucous Nat King Cole Trio, though his own taste was soon to be for the wilder styles of Jackie Wilson, Fats Domino, Ray Charles and Little Richard. His growing collection had a sizeable input of R&B records.

The lyrics to Border Song, with its declamatory 'Holy Moses' and plea for release, cried out for a gospel treatment. In verdant Middlesex, Elton managed to evoke the distant black music hubs of Detroit, Michigan, and Muscle Shoals, Alabama. It was a convincing enough facsimile to be recorded that same year by Dorothy Morrison, who sang on Oh Happy Day with the Edwin Hawkins Singers, and by the soul diva herself, Aretha Franklin. Aretha's version reached number thirty-seven on the Billboard chart, which made it her joint least successful single at that point. But just to be recorded by her was thrill enough for Bernie and Elton.

The sentiment of the song was a plea for racial harmony despite hostile surroundings, a message that resonated strongly in an America still convulsed by the Civil Rights and Black Power movements. A sparse piano opening is followed by the unadorned voice of Elton as soul brother number one. The following verse brings in the strings; with the chorus comes a short burst of choir followed by a nicely-placed rock beat. All is meticulously crafted and arranged, signalling in spirit if not style what was to come on the album under the influence of producer Gus Dudgeon and arranger Paul Buckmaster.

Steve Brown hired Buckmaster to arrange Elton's songs, realising that his own experience as a producer did not extend to coping with a sixty-piece orchestra and a professional recording studio. Due to Dick James' connections with The

Border Song

Beatles, Brown was able to approach George Martin. But Martin would only agree if he could do the arrangements as well. Instead, Brown was impressed enough with Buckmaster's ideas to take his advice and hire his colleague Gus Dudgeon, who'd worked on David Bowie's Space Oddity, a single that reached number five in September 1969.

Gus Dudgeon trained as an engineer with Decca, before having four hit singles in quick succession with different acts, including Bowie and The Bonzo Dog Doo Dah Band's I'm the Urban Spaceman. Steve Brown brought Bernie and Elton with him to Dudgeon's office. Without an introduction, Dudgeon was under the illusion for the first half-hour that the rock star-looking Bernie was actually Elton. Brown was furious after the meeting because he thought Dudgeon was unimpressed with the demos, and here was he making the supreme sacrifice of giving up Elton. Dudgeon saw it differently, saying he was excited but was trying to be cool, fearing over-enthusiasm would lose him the job. After flitting between singles acts, Dudgeon was keen to develop a long-term artist, and he was sure Elton John was the one. Elton's voice reminded Dudgeon of Jose

Feliciano, who had recently had a hit with a smoochy version of The Doors Light My Fire. (Feliciano himself would soon record Take Me To The Pilot and Border Song and, as Elton observed, begin to sound like him.)

Dudgeon negotiated a generous fee and royalty for himself with Dick James and said he needed a big budget to get the album right. To Brown's amazement, this ploy secured unlimited funds from Dick James. At £6,000 the album ended up costing about three times the average for an unknown artist.

Dudgeon and Buckmaster returned to the 16-track Trident Studios where they had recorded Bowie. Located in St Anne's Court, Soho, it was a few minutes both from Dudgeon's office on Oxford Street and the Dick James Studio. The Dudgeon-Buckmaster partnership adopted their now familiar approach. It was the sound Elton was after. Buckmaster was also keen to experiment with the fizzy sounds of the new Moog synthesiser and use it in tandem with strings. After a discussion with Elton about how he saw the songs, Dudgeon and Buckmaster would adjourn. The pair would repeatedly play the demos, both putting in ideas as cello player Buckmaster meticulously scored arrangements for the full orchestra they were to bring in to the studio. As on Space Oddity, they wanted everything planned so carefully that only one interpretation was possible in the studio.

Most of the album was recorded in a week at the rate of three sessions a day with the orchestra from ten until two, four until six, and seven until ten, sticking to Buckmaster and Dudgeon's tightly-organised schedule. The first time Elton heard the arrangements was in the studio as he was playing them. He had to muster all his scholarly resources to make sure he didn't fluff the score with the orchestra.

No-one saw Border Song as a potential hit. Indeed, Elton soon referred to it as Boredom Song. But it was accessible and up-tempo, and a good sampler for the album. Like Lady Samantha, it received reasonable airplay and fulfilled its function of rekindling limited interest in Elton John. In his days as session all comer, he had appeared on *Top of the Pops* as a back-up piano player for less-than-credible pop acts Pickettywitch and Brotherhood Of Man. With Border Song, he was able finally to appear in his own right – though that didn't help the song infiltrate the charts. 🄴🄹

Your Song

Your Song

Recorded: January 1970, Trident Studios, St Anne's Court, London
First released: Elton John album, April 1970

AS A LOVESTRUCK TEENAGER, Bernie Taupin would often have a hit of the week. Maybe it would be Del Shannon, or Gene Pitney, whose song and voice would put into words his personal drama relating to the often unknowing object of his affections. He was still a teenager, just, when he went to live with Elton and his mother and stepfather. It was over a breakfast of scrambled eggs that Bernie wrote a song which neatly portrays the contortions of the lovestruck: the desire to perform heroic deeds and give a token of affection, in this case the song itself. Bernie later confessed that Your Song was the frustrated outpourings of a reluctant virgin. Elton was convinced the song was for a girl with glasses from Lincolnshire whom Bernie had been seeing and who resembled Greek chanteuse Nana Mouskouri. It's a version Bernie disputes, saying the song is about no-one in particular.

Elton expressed his own yearnings and insecurities in his melodic interpretation of the lyrics. His original demo of Your Song was slightly up-tempo of what would become the classic. It had a pounding pub piano and was a bit too cheery for the sentiments. Even so, everyone who heard it sensed the song's special quality. Everyone except Elton, who to this day can never recognise a hit.

Here, however, was the breakthrough song needed to launch Elton John as a star in Britain and America. But it had to wait until January 1971, nine months after the release of the Elton John album and three months after the release of the subsequent album Tumbleweed Connection. It was only reluctantly put out by Dick James when he was forced to follow its success in America, where Elton was signed to a subsidiary of the giant MCA, a company James had no influence over.

America warmed to Elton far more quickly than Britain. In August 1970 he had played a week's residency in Los Angeles at celebrated folk venue the Troubadour Club, to promote the Elton John album, and was hailed as the new musical messiah. He was introduced on stage by Neil Diamond and lauded by critics and cognoscenti such as Quincy Jones, the Beach Boys, Randy Newman, Graham Nash, Bread and even Gordon Lightfoot. His album reached number four in America. In Britain, it briefly peaked at number eleven, his first record chart placing. Your Song reached number eight on the Billboard chart in America and number seven in Great Britain.

The arrangement for Your Song allowed Elton's sensitive character to breathe, starting with a simple piano introduction, then a verse with piano followed by orchestral strings. As the song builds, the guitar picks out the tune. By the fourth verse, it is time for the drums to emphasise the beat followed by a full orchestral sweep. All the time, Elton's voice retains its moderation emphasising emotional intensity. Everything builds to the last verse and climax where the ensemble reach a brief crescendo. It was a skilfully measured performance.

As the opening song on the album, Your Song positioned Elton as a pop balladeer. It was not representative of the wide stylistic range that was to follow in his career. The general impression among music critics at the time was that a thoughtful artist was emerging. The poetic bent of lyrics such as No Shoestrings On Louise and The King Must Die seemed to confirm that Elton was about meaningful if convoluted poetry and rich melodic textures. He would have been sniffily dismissed if he was perceived as an extrovert showman.

The album cover, featuring Elton's pensive face in shadowy light emerging from the dark background, all added to the impression that here was an introvert. The line-up on the back cover was a snapshot of some of the major players in Elton's life at that point. Elton was standing between Paul Buckmaster and Bernie. There was Gus Dudgeon, Caleb Quaye and Steve Brown, credited as co-ordinator. On Buckmaster's other side, was his girlfriend and later wife Diana Lewis, credited with playing Moog. All tried out their best cool look. EJ

Your Song

Take Me To The Pilot

Recorded: January 1970, Trident Studios, St Anne's Court, London
First released: Elton John album, 10 April, 1970

THERE ARE ECHOES OF TENNYSON, Macauley, Coleridge, Sir Walter Scott and Corinthians; of a heroic adventurer crossing the great divide on the soul's great journey, putting away childish things to look through a glass darkly. Or maybe not. It could just be a random juxtaposition of words, as Bernie has stated, though the lyrics of Take Me To The Pilot do reflect a love for the very sound of words. Bernie made rather grandiose references at the time to the cut-up practices copied by David Bowie and the experimentation of Baudelaire and Rimbaud. He had also been reading the more popular science fiction of Michael Moorcock.

As a child, Bernie's mother read him classic narrative poetry (such as *The Ancient Mariner*) and Take Me To The Pilot makes a little sense as a plea to be taken to the pilot who controls the soul, a desire for enlightenment and experience. The imagery of a pilot is a useful narrative device as well as an ancient one.

It makes the song all the more remarkable that, when faced with these incomprehensible verses, Elton could make a great tune out of it. The lyrics have a natural rhythm which Elton takes as his guide. The natural staccato of the short lines is ideal for the piano-bashing rhythm and blues and honky-tonk he employs.

Ever-present is the influence of Leon Russell, an idol for Elton at the time, in whose early 1970s recordings can be heard so much of what Elton was to become as a singer and piano player. Russell (who also learned classical piano as a child) played with Jerry Lee Lewis, Phil Spector and Joe Cocker, though it was his work with Delaney and Bonnie that was the strongest influence for Elton. Their mix of Southern soul-rock, funk and country can be most strongly felt on Tumbleweed Connection.

After Russell saw Elton play at the Troubadour he invited him to jam at his home studio in Los Angeles the following day. Within a few months Elton was to share equal billing with Russell at New York's Fillmore East and they were to

Take Me To The Pilot

play on stage together. Russell told Elton he'd written Delta Lady after hearing one of Elton and Bernie's songs and expressed a desire to record Border Song.

The Elton who first started recording was withdrawn and averse to the idea of playing live, perhaps because of his punishing touring experiences with Bluesology, criss-crossing the country to get to three gigs a night. He'd had to be convinced that, as well as airplay, live performance was needed to stimulate public curiosity. He formed a band with bass player Dee Murray and drummer Nigel Olsson from the disbanded Spencer Davis Group. He saw no need for a guitarist. Their first gig was supporting pianist Sergio Mendes, the bossa nova king, in Paris, where they had cabbages and coins thrown at them. The first British gig was at the Pop Proms in the hippie sanctum of London's Roundhouse. They'd played just fifteen British dates by the time they reached Los Angeles and the Troubadour. The meek former parcel packer was soon packing a punchy keyboard, kicking away his piano stool and dressing in flamboyant clothes. Take Me To The Pilot was one of the showier songs he performed, allowing the hitherto suppressed side of his nature to flourish. His shows on that first tour of America were all to receive standing ovations. The recorded version of the song sounded restrained by comparison.

Come Down In Time

Recorded: March 1970, Trident Studios, London
First released: Tumbleweed Connection album, October 1970

STILL CITED BY ELTON JOHN AS ONE of his favourite songs, Come Down In Time
was first recorded using the session group rhythm section. Arranger Paul
Buckmaster, on hearing the result, suggested he might be able to improve
on it. Elton considered Buckmaster a genius, even if he was repelled by
his less than fastidious personal habits (such as leaving bits of breakfast over
the score). So if Buckmaster wanted to have a go, no one was going to
question his judgement.

   Most of the songs on Tumbleweed Connection were written at the same time
as those for the Elton John album, but set aside as being stylistically distinct.
The new album's style was dictated largely by the Old West themes of Bernie's
songs, which lent themselves to country, folk and funky soul. The emphasis was

Come Down In Time

on a stripped-down sound though Come Down In Time was an exception, harking back to the lushness of the earlier record.

Buckmaster's arrangement opens with a solo harp motif introducing Elton's voice, set against a delicate acoustic guitar followed by simple bass and piano lines. The percussion kicks in the rock beat as an oboe delicately evokes the lovelorn theme of the lyrics. It is the rock equivalent of a demure chamber orchestra. As the intensity of the song builds, the more symphonic and syncopated it becomes. The strings join in, retreat for the chorus, and then repeat the original theme as the song abruptly ends.

The story of a stood-up lover who came down to meet the object of his desire in time, only to find she was not there, is one of Bernie's most successful lyrically. Every word evokes the clandestine nature of the never-to-be encounter, set against the gloomy backdrop, the birdsong of the nightjars and the image of the moon and mantle of light from the room.

Elton's recording deal with DJM stipulated that he should release two albums a year, which was relatively commonplace in an era before release dates were fixed with strategic precision. Aware that other groups had got into trouble by not fulfilling their contracts, Elton was keen to honour his obligations and, two months after recording the first album, he was back in Trident Studios.

Tumbleweed was not recorded in as seamless a way as its predecessor. Several tracks were re-recorded. Mostly present were the original Hookfoot nucleus of Quaye, Pope, bass player Dave Glover and harmonica player Ian Duck. It also saw the first appearance on tape of drummer Nigel Olsson and bass player Dee Murray. Their first appearance on vinyl was the track Amoreena, despite the protestations of Gus Dudgeon who thought their playing was not up to it. Elton insisted and regarded the track, influenced by Van Morrison, as his favourite.

Recording for Tumbleweed started before the release of Elton John and thus was not influenced by the reception of that album. If it had been, Buckmaster might have been encouraged to do more to increase its commercial appeal. Though individual tracks received decent airplay no single was released from Tumbleweed. It all helped inadvertently build the credibility of Elton John. Having Tumbleweed in your collection, with its beautifully intricate sleeve and inserts, was hip in 1970.

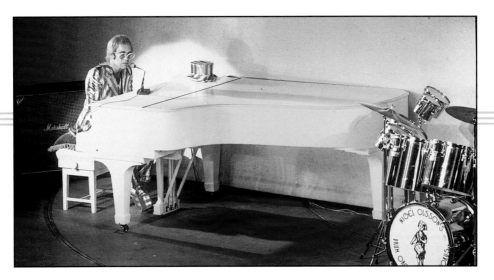

Burn Down The Mission
Recorded: March 1970, Trident Studios, London
First released: Tumbleweed Connection album, October 1970

BERNIE TAUPIN WAS DRAWN TO THE LAND that he grew up on around Maltkins Farm, Owmsby-by-Spital, Lincolnshire. He would have passionate debates with his new friend from the city, espousing his love of the fenlands of eastern England and the countryside in general. He wanted to hang on to a country way of life while desperate to explore America, the land of his dreams.

In their first year of meeting, Bernie would bring with him bundles of lyrics that he penned in the isolation of home. When he finally moved to London to facilitate the songwriting process, he was instantly nostalgic for his roots. Intertwined with his memories of a rural, idyllic childhood was his fascination with America's Old West; the Alamo, the Civil War, the rugged pioneers and outlaws. Like Elton, he was first drawn to folk, blues and country and western through Lonnie Donegan, a Glaswegian who faked an American sound and launched the peculiarly British skiffle boom, with its tea-chest basses and washboard percussion. Bernie's cousin played him Donegan's version of old spirituals, John Henry's Hammer and Pick A Bale Of Cotton.

Bernie was not so impressed when Donegan became more commercial and scored a hit with Rock Island Line. However, when Bernie realised the song was written by the bruising black bluesman Huddie 'Leadbelly' Ledbetter he went to the source, discovering along the way Leadbelly's fellow pioneer in raw dustbowl folk, Woody Guthrie.

Bernie was also drawn to a more romantic and saccharine version of the American West via Marty Robbins and his album Trail Songs And Gunfighter Ballads, and in particular the tune El Paso. Its account of the sweet Mexican girl from the west Texas town was a revelation. Here was a real story with characters that could be conveyed in song. Bernie would pay tribute to the song throughout his career.

By the time his songwriting partnership with Elton was flowering, Bernie

Burn Down The Mission

worshipped at the altar of Bob Dylan and his sometime backing group The Band. Their album Music From The Big Pink, the songwriting of Robbie Robertson and The Band's celebration of simple American ways, American folklore and innovative narrative style were fresh in his mind when he was writing Tumbleweed Connection.

It was Elton who at first seemed more passionate about contemporary America, and more likely to move there. He loved black music and the West Coast elite of Crosby, Stills, Nash and Young, Joni Mitchell, James Taylor, Jefferson Airplane and, crucially, The Beach Boys. He, too, loved The Band, in particular their song The Weight. Elton told one interviewer he felt more American than British. He was itching to get to the States and raid a record store; it would save waiting for the latest expensive imports from his favourite shops in London's Soho.

On Tumbleweed Connection the songs are mostly fantasies about Americana, an expression of Bernie's feelings towards a country he was yet to visit. There were stories about guns and old soldiers, a fugitive, the American Civil War and rural life. Burn Down The Mission was classed by Bernie as one of his 'dramatics'. It's the story of the struggle between rich and poor, the setting purposefully vague, a mission somewhere in pioneer country. He had to deny crass accusations that it was an exhortation to political violence. Starting in a gospel vein, by the time it reaches the chorus the funk builds, followed by a quickening tempo. A blast of brass with strings is used to calm things down for the middle eight. In turns stroking and cajoling, the song builds into a boogie anthem and was to become for Elton John concerts what Street Fighting Man was for the Rolling Stones. The song closed the album and for some time would be used to close live shows. With its innovative TV advertising, continued radio support and the British sitting up in response to American attention, Tumbleweed Connection was the first Elton John album to reach the Top Ten, staying in the charts for five months. The sepia-coloured cover shot in a railway station on the Bluebell Line in West Sussex was an attempt to reflect the historical themes of many of the songs, even if the British advertising hoardings for Cadbury's chocolate, Swan Vestas and the *Daily Telegraph* would have been very unfamiliar in the Old West.

The finest accolade for Bernie came when his greatest heroes The Band and Bob Dylan turned up to see Elton perform at the Fillmore East in New York. So impressed were The Band, they delayed a gig in upstate New York to fly down to Philadelphia to catch the show. Meeting backstage afterwards, Elton and Bernie played them Tumbleweed Connection, two months before its release in America. According to Elton they went berserk. Robbie Robertson asked them to write a song for The Band and record at their legendary Woodstock studio. EJ

Madman Across The Water

Madman Across The Water
Recorded: August 1971, Trident Studios, London
First released: Madman Across The Water album, November 1971

THE CRITICAL BACKLASH AGAINST Elton John had begun. Music writers realised that maybe he wasn't the owlish performer he had at first seemed. There were the rather flamboyant little touches to the outfits he was wearing on stage, like his Mickey Mouse ears at a Disneyland show. A live album, 17-11-70, recorded at a New York radio station in front of a small audience, was a bit too lively for the dour temperament of the arbiters of taste. Though mauled by the press, 17-11-70 displayed the maturity, ease and vocal and instrumental dexterity that allowed Elton to rise so swiftly. Performing necessarily simplified versions of Take Me To The Pilot and Burn Down The Mission with his touring band of Olsson and Murray, what the album lacked in studio smoothness it gained in unfettered verve.

The live album was released to forestall bootleggers. It pre-empted by a month the release of Friends, a movie soundtrack with five songs written by Elton and Bernie. They had been contracted to write it when their career had hit a lull prior to the life-changing Troubadour experience and was completed on their return. The album was padded out with lacklustre Buckmaster arrangements. Friends, released on the Paramount label in the US and ABC in the UK, crowded out the market in Elton John vinyl. Like the British film it accompanied, it was poorly received.

Soon after these two albums were released, Elton and Bernie were back at Trident Studios to record Madman Across The Water. The atmosphere was tense. The usual stockpile of songs had been exhausted, an intense touring schedule had not allowed enough time for Bernie and Elton to maintain their previous output of three songs a week.

The studio mood for Madman was not enhanced by Paul Buckmaster turning up at the studio having forgotten his score and being forced to send home sixty session musicians waiting to record the title track. Buckmaster was brought back in an attempt to recapture some of the Elton John album flourishes.

Elton himself stormed out after a furious row with Dick James over some re-recording. He stayed away for a week until his new manager (and boyfriend, although only Elton's closest friends knew at the time) John Reid, former UK label boss at Tamla Motown Records, prevailed upon him.

Bernie could at least finally write about an America he had visited extensively while accompanying Elton on tour. The result was a more varied view of the country in songs like Indian Sunset; as near as he got to a protest song highlighting the third-class-citizen status of what are now called Native Americans. Rotten Peaches mentioned cocaine and pills and a home that was ten thousand miles away, seen through the eyes of a captive. Taupin mostly loved what he saw of America, and enjoyed cruising the LA freeways with the radio on. He wrote about his new girlfriend and wife-to-be Maxine Feibelman, whom he met in Los Angeles (she is the object of desire in the song Tiny Dancer).

On Madman, Bernie conjured up the insanity of an asylum inmate on visiting day. Elton's instincts called for a guitar arrangement on the song. As there was no guitarist in the band, producer Gus Dudgeon first looked to Michael Chapman, a folk artist with a bleak style with whom he was working on another project. Chapman was required to play chords in harmonics, a job he executed skilfully. After Chapman's session however, it was decided to try an electric guitar. For this, Dudgeon brought in another player he had worked with, Mick Ronson of David Bowie's Spiders From Mars. Ronson's feeble psychedelic version can be heard on the Rare Masters album released in 1992.

Finally, it was decided to combine acoustic and electric guitar and after Chapman declined another session, having found the first too stressful, in came another musician Dudgeon had worked with, Davey Johnstone, an acoustic guitarist from folk group Magna Carta, along with Johnstone's colleague Rick Wakeman on organ. The electric guitar part was filled by session man Chris Spedding. Percussionist Ray Cooper, later to become one of Elton's closest friends, made his first appearance. Buckmaster's orchestration was added later.

Madman was a chart failure, reaching only forty-one in the UK. It was slated by the critics, and Elton wished he could re-record his vocals on Tiny Dancer, Blues For My Baby and Levon. Like Tumbleweed, the album lacked natural singles and none were released in Britain. Tiny Dancer and Levon were released in America but gained low chart positions. But it was not an artistic failure. The Buckmaster arrangements are less showy and more sympathetic to the LP's downbeat tone, while Indian Sunset and Levon would be considered strong ballads in any era. EJ

Rocket Man

Rocket Man (I Think It's Going to Be a Long, Long Time)

Recorded: January 1972, Strawberry Studios, Château d'Hierouville, France
First released: c/w Holiday Inn, Goodbye, April 1972

AS BERNIE TAUPIN HIT THE BEND in the road on that star-filled night close to his parents' home in the Lincolnshire countryside, the opening lines came to him. Arriving home, he dashed into the house gesturing that he did not want to be disturbed. He had the words of the entire song in his head and had to write them down before his fitful memory allowed them to disappear into the ether.

It was zero hour and the song lifted off. Its origins were not entirely Bernie's invention. The title, Rocket Man, was the same as a despairing song by the sensitive American folk artist Tom Rapp, recorded by his group Pearls Before Swine. The theme was familiar enough.

Bernie admitted to another source of inspiration for Rocket Man: A Day In The Life Of A Tree was written by Brian Wilson of The Beach Boys with their then manager Jack Rieley, who had encouraged the group to write more credible lyrics. The song appeared on their 1971 album Surf's Up. It is a simplistic ode to the beauty of trees and nature sapped by pollution, performed in a style that Bernie termed 'spacey', and which inspired the mood if not the musical theme of Rocket Man.

The astronaut in question is pining for his wife. Beneath the veneer of heroism he feels lonely and dejected. It is a fine example of Bernie's sleight of hand. Superficially, Rocket Man is intrepid and gung-ho as astronauts were deemed to be in those days of NASA near-infallibility and regular Apollo missions. Only on closer inspection is the rocket man as imperfect as his fellow man. And, yes, the reference to being high as a kite does allude to drug use as much as heavenly altitude.

Elton's skill was exactly to mirror the conflicting themes. The 'rocket man' chorus gives the feel of starry-eyed exploration and is almost anthemic in its reach. Yet the underlying mood, accentuated by the blue overtones of the key of B flat in which the song is composed, is one of overwhelming sadness. Dudgeon was careful not to use Buckmaster strings, thus avoiding too close a comparison with the pair's earlier masterpiece (Space Oddity). For the space effects

Dudgeon made subtle use of an ARP synthesiser played by the studio engineer, David Hentschel. There is an ease and a new pop sensibility about this song that marks a turning point in the Taupin–John songwriting partnership. Bernie had adopted a simpler, more straightforward form of lyric writing. Gaining in self-confidence, he was no longer as intent on proving his poetic credentials. On the album's opening track, Honky Cat, he was not too self-conscious to rhyme 'get back' with 'honky cat'. In the song Slave he rhymes 'land', 'hand', 'stand' and 'can' while most compositions on the album have regular metres.

After four albums without singles or singles chart success, Rocket Man became only Elton's second British hit, reaching number two, while in the United States it got to number six. The energy of the album and Elton's ability to cast off the negative forces that had recently beset him – notably when he feared he was close to a nervous breakdown after too much intensive touring – was to become a regular feature of his career. 🎹

Mona Lisas And Mad Hatters

Mona Lisas And Mad Hatters
Recorded: January 1972, Strawberry Studios, Château d'Hierouville, France
First released: Honky Chateau album, May 1972

HAVING REACHED MILLIONAIRE STATUS the previous year, thanks to touring and a new record deal with MCA in America, Elton was advised by his accountants to spend time out of Britain to avoid the then punitive income tax rates. Gus Dudgeon first tried to rent the Rolling Stones Mobile in the South of France to record a new album, but the Stones themselves were using it. His second option was a harebrained scheme to build his own temporary studio by renting a villa in the South of France and padding out rooms with scores of mattresses to baffle the noise and avoid structural damage. Dudgeon met up with John Reid to check out a few residences. The scheme was soon abandoned as impractical. Meanwhile Dudgeon heard mention of Strawberry Studios, which was part of a chateau in the countryside 40 kilometres north of Paris. The studio at the 17th century Château d'Hierouville had previously been used by the Grateful Dead and, after an inspection, Dudgeon deemed it fairly basic but suitable.

It was important to write as well as record abroad if full benefit was to be made of the tax breaks. Ensconced with his new wife Maxine, Bernie set up a conveyor belt system of writing with Elton. Bernie would write the lyrics. Maxine would type them out and correct the spelling. She would deliver them downstairs to Elton at his piano at one end of a long conservatory-type room, running the length of one wall in the chateau. Within minutes out popped the tunes and Elton would be playing them with the band which was at hand.

Mona Lisas And Mad Hatters was an exception. The lyrics were written during Bernie and Elton's first visit to New York in September 1970 following the Troubadour appearances. A man had been shot outside their hotel in midtown Manhattan on the day they arrived and the song was written the day after. In it Bernie refers to the difference between his old romantic view of America and New York City and the reality with which he would soon become familiar. It is a celebration of the diversity and vivacity of New York as well as its hazards (the subway is punnily referred to as a place no good man deserved to go down). Bernie kissed the ground the first day he arrived in America and his heart has never left. He is now an American citizen.

Elton's rendition of Mona Lisas is suffused with that sense of wonderment and warmth for the most vibrant city in the world. Davey Johnstone's mandolin adds an ethnic flavour and the overall effect is of an affectionate tribute.

Bernie tried to paint a more upbeat picture of the city with Mona Lisas And Mad Hatters (Part 2) in 1988 on the Reg Strikes Back album. Neither the lyrics nor the music is up to the standard of the original. This Mona Lisa is older, presumably wiser and maybe more jaded. Even Bernie had learnt to look over the bag people as he walked and observed the city. Elton gave it a plodding jazz funk melody only enlivened by the trumpet and flugelhorn breaks of Freddie Hubbard.

Honky Chateau was the first time the new line-up featuring Davey Johnstone was fully constituted. Johnstone's background had been solely in acoustic instruments, and his first tentative recording on electric guitar on the honky tonk Susie (Dramas) is a stilted and sad affair, though the song is carefree and reflects Elton's sunnier mood during the recording. I Think I'm Going To Kill Myself has Elton doing his best pub jangle piano routine, with a glorious tap dance from 'Legs' Larry Smith of the Bonzo Dog Doo Dah Band turning the faux morbid lyrics into a giant laugh. Devoid of Buckmaster strings and with sparse contributions from a French horn section arranged by Dudgeon, and the electric violin of Jean-Luc Ponty, the overall mood of the album is fresh and celebratory.

Spurred on by the success of the single Rocket Man, Honky Chateau became Elton's first American number one, staying on top for five weeks. In Britain it reached the top three, his highest position to date. Before recording the album Elton had aired his doubts as to whether he would enjoy a long career. Those doubts could now be banished.

Mona Lisas And Mad Hatters

Crocodile Rock
Recorded: June 1972, Strawberry Studios, Château d'Hierouville, France
First released: c/w Elderberry Wine, October 1972

AT THE NORTHWOOD HILLS HOTEL (in reality a pub, despite its grand name), the barely teenage Reg Dwight would stab out music hall favourites like My Old Man Said Follow The Van and the cheesy American country ballads of 'Gentleman'

Crocodile Rock

Jim Reeves. The soundtrack to his private listening pleasure was more adventurous than he dared test on the pub clientele. He was an enthusiast for every heartthrob, piano thumper, falsetto, twister and raver thrown up by the American Dream. The nearest he got to them was caressing their discs before they spun on his turntable, or viewing British pretenders like Billy Fury when he arrived at the Harrow Granada, a few stops down on the Tube.

Bill Haley's See You Later Alligator, and its rejoinder, 'In a while, Crocodile' (a catchphrase for 1950s bobby-soxers), was the inspiration for Bernie's lyrics to Crocodile Rock. It was as intentionally obvious as the musical pastiche of late 1950s and early 1960s hits conjured up by Elton.

High on Elton's list in the pre-Beatles early 1960s were Del Shannon and Bobby Vee, who inspired the vocals for the song. Neil Sedaka, whose career in a few years would gain a second wind on Elton's Rocket Records label, was also there with his Oh Carol. So was Pat Boone's Speedy Gonzales (though its writers were not flattered and sued for plagiarism, later dropping the action).

In the background there is a guitar riff from Dream Lover by Bobby Darin. And there's Eddie Cochran, plus Little Darlin' from The Diamonds, some Freddy Cannon and some Beach Boys. The Beach Boys acknowledged their own influence by performing the song on the 1992 Elton John tribute album Two Rooms. The organ at the beginning pays homage to the Farfisa sound of Johnny and the Hurricanes. During the recording there was an attempt to slip in a Duane Eddy guitar twang, but it didn't work, though Davey Johnstone's competence on the electric guitar had rapidly matured and he was successfully mimicking various rock 'n' roll styles.

Elton was happy to own up to the song being derivative of an era that had ended just nine years before it was written. His intention was to reflect the music he grew up with.

The mood of Crocodile Rock did not reflect the way Elton was feeling at the time of writing. Arriving at the chateau in June 1972 for the Don't Shoot Me I'm Only The Piano Player sessions, he should have been buoyed by the news that Honky Chateau had gone to number one in America. Instead he was on the verge of a nervous breakdown, not realising until later that he was suffering from glandular fever. Elton told Dudgeon he did not feel capable of making the album. Dudgeon said they should reconvene in September. On reconsideration, Elton felt he would enjoy his forthcoming holiday with the album out of the way, and so decided to go ahead after all.

Elton and Bernie had three songs left over from Honky Chateau and wrote twelve more in two days. While a happy atmosphere had previously surrounded the making of Honky Chateau, here there was just stress.

The quality of the album is remarkable for such a rushed project. As well as the classic Crocodile Rock and Daniel there were other commendable numbers: I'm Gonna Be A Teenage Idol inspired by Bernie and Elton's friend and glam rock star Marc Bolan, with its brassy, saccharine pop; the tense, fluid riffs of Have Mercy On The Criminal; throwaway stompers like Teacher I Need You and Midnight Creeper. Ironically, Elton, who regarded himself as a veteran, became a teenage idol with this album, finding himself being screamed at by hordes of teenage girls.

Perhaps feeling guilty at executing the album so quickly, Elton didn't rate it highly, thinking it disposable pop. But then he always considered pop songs disposable: like postage stamps, one lick and they are gone. Having already suffered the vagaries of the critics with poor grace, he expected to be buried for the album. Instead he was praised.

The somewhat defensive Don't Shoot Me I'm Only The Piano Player title came out of Elton's response to continued ribbing from Groucho Marx, whom he had befriended in Los Angeles. Groucho insisted that Elton John was using his name the wrong way round. Groucho's influence was obliquely honoured on the album cover, a 1950s scene of a boy and girl buying tickets at a street cinema booth for a performance of Don't Shoot Me starring Elton John. Advertised as a future attraction is The Marx Brothers film *Go West*.

Daniel

Daniel

Recorded: June 1972, Strawberry Studios, Château d'Hierouville, France
First released: c/w Skyline Pigeon and Don't Shoot Me I'm Only The Piano Player
album, both January 1973

THE MISSING VERSE TO DANIEL is a continuing conundrum that Bernie Taupin
refuses to solve. For a man who fastidiously keeps copies of his original lyrics and
chronicles, Daniel is the one song that seems to have escaped his curatorial
tendencies. The last verse of the song was lopped off by Elton. It is believed to be
the verse that would enable its meaning to become clear though at the time Elton
thought his abridged version was self-explanatory and was perplexed at the fuss.
He later recanted and admitted that the missing verse explained everything.

The three extant verses refer to Daniel who we know is travelling to Spain and
saying goodbye to his brother. Daniel has witnessed something so terrible that the
pain will not heal and so he is leaving his homeland to seek refuge in the most
beautiful place he has ever seen.

The cryptic lyrics left everything to the imagination. One early conjecture which
Elton and Bernie found hilarious was that it was about a homosexual relationship,
particularly since it was suggested by a skinhead in Manchester. Another clue
comes from Gus Dudgeon who reckons 'a ship's dog named Paul' may form part
of the missing verse, though this sounds out of character with the rest of the song,

and Bernie has no recollection of it. Daniel was inspired by an article Bernie had read in *Newsweek* magazine about veterans returning from the Vietnam War. He wrote down the lyrics in the magazine's margins. Bernie has given different versions of Daniel's meaning. In one, Daniel was a one-eyed and, in another, a crippled Vietnam vet, injured in the Tet offensive, coming home to a small town in Texas. The story relates the conflict between a community that wished to laud its homecoming hero and the veteran's desire to return to an inconspicuous farm life. Daniel was important for Bernie, because it was the only song he'd written about Vietnam, and though containing no political comment, it makes a simple, safe observation about the dislocation of war which was sympathetic to the people who returned home.

Verse changes were rarely a source of conflict between Elton and Bernie, who takes care never to put too strident a message in Elton's mouth or to bare his soul too starkly. Convoluted attempts at concealment may explain why he has strayed so often into obtuse lyrics and lain himself open to charges of pretentiousness.

If Elton played the missing verse to Dudgeon in rehearsal, according to Dudgeon's recollection, then it was deleted before the time came to lay down the track in the studio. The tune's defining sound is the flute effect on the Mellotron, a keyboard-based instrument that was the forerunner to the modern sampler with its tape loop of effects, played here by Elton. It has two strong melody lines played separately in verse and chorus with the secondary melody in the background on the final chorus. The effect is to lodge the catchy, hummable melodies in the mind through repetition. It was a massive hit.

On this occasion Elton believed that he had actually written a hit. Not so Dick James, however, who was unconvinced of the commercial potential of ballads, even though he had been a balladeer himself in the 1950s. Elton and James' relationship had been deteriorating for a while. They had argued during the recording of Don't Shoot Me and ended up not talking for four months. It was during these sessions that the idea to set up Rocket Records was formed.

Dick James had his way over Daniel, making Crocodile Rock the first single to be released from Don't Shoot Me. He relented finally but refused to pay for any advertising to promote Daniel. Elton was furious that James was willing to take the profits while unwilling to invest in the song, though when it became a hit James agreed to absorb the costs. The momentum in Elton's career was heading towards climax as he had his second hit in six months. Daniel reached number four in the UK and number two in America. 🎹

Saturday Night's Alright For Fighting

Saturday Night's Alright For Fighting

Recorded: May 1973, Strawberry Studios, Château d'Hierouville, France
First released: c/w Jack Rabbit, Whenever You're Ready (We'll Go Steady Again), June 1973

LEGAL PROBLEMS OVER OWNERSHIP of Strawberry Studios at the Chateau d'Hierouville meant it was out of bounds for what Elton and Co. hoped would be their third successful album emanating from the French countryside. Looking for another location to escape the British taxman, Elton heard that Roberta Flack had recorded Killing Me Softly in Jamaica, and that the Rolling Stones had just finished recording Goat's Head Soup at the island's Dynamic

Sound Studios. It all sounded fun. Plus, he liked reggae.

The Elton John party arrived on 23 January 1973, the day after a Joe Frazier versus George Foreman world championship boxing match. Kingston was buzzing with excitable fans who added to the capital's menacing air.

Byron Lee's Dynamic Sound Studios, in a compound that also housed a record company and record pressing plant, was protected by guards armed with machine guns barring entry to striking pickets. When Elton and the band arrived in their open-windowed bus they could feel the breath of the pickets blowing on their faces with blow pipes. When several people subsequently came out in rashes they surmised that the pickets had been blowing crushed fibre glass. It was an inauspicious precursor of things to come.

The studio equipment, including the piano, were of a poor standard. Gus Dudgeon found it impossible to get a decent sound. Terrified to go out of his room at the Pink Flamingo Hotel, Elton caressed his Fender Rhodes electric piano as Bernie wrote in his own bedroom. Elton set twenty-one lyrics to music, four more than were used on the album, in the space of two days. He and Bernie remained in Kingston despite the band inadvertently being booked into a hotel in Ocho Rios, a calmer resort across the island.

When news came through that Don't Shoot Me I'm Only The Piano Player had reached number one in Britain and America, the band celebrated in the Pink Flamingo's dining room. Elton had remained in his room, ruminating about the studio problems, when he made a sudden appearance among the band and crew, a sheet covering his nakedness, fleeing a giant centipede that had strolled over him.

Saturday Night's Alright For Fighting was the only track recorded at Dynamic Sounds after two and a half days of trying. The end result sounded as if it was being played through tin cans. Dudgeon was baffled and everyone put it down to 'the vibes'. Thereafter the studio was abandoned and several disputatious days were spent trying to get a flight out of the island after the group's equipment and cars were impounded in an argument over who should be paying the hotel bill, them or, as they had imagined, the recording studio. Elton was convinced he was going to be murdered when the taxi driver taking

Saturday Night's Alright For Fighting

him to the airport drove through a sugar cane field. Fleeing to New York, they received word that the chateau was now available.

The original recording of Saturday Night's Alright was abandoned. Back in the chateau, nearly everything went smoothly. Up to five songs were recorded in one day. The album took fifteen days in all, their longest yet.

Even at the chateau though, they found it hard to get Saturday Night's Alright perfect. The problem lay in Elton's desire to make it a guitar-led as opposed to piano-led track. In the end he decided to record the band first – screaming obscenities at the band to wind them up – then the piano and finally the vocals. He found it hard to adjust to singing without his usual props. Standing up in the studio felt strange. His solution was to leap around like a madman.

The traditional Saturday night punch-up, often preceded by a sing-song, is a quaint British tradition. Teenage Reg was always terrified that fights would break out during the three years he performed his Friday, Saturday and Sunday-night stints at the Northwood Hills pub. If the adolescent Bernie had visited the pub he might have joined in any rumpus. His behaving badly period occurred around the time that he was working on a chicken farm and playing a lot of snooker, drinking a lot of beer and staying out all night. Saturday Night's Alright is intended to be an English working class pub song. There's mention of a bellyful of beer and laddish 1960s vernacular: 'aggravation', 'dolly' and 'oiled'. Bernie wanted to honour the British culture he had abandoned.

Elton the pop star and balladeer reasserted himself as a rock 'n' roller. He saw Saturday Night's Alright appealing to diehard Elton John fans, whereas ballads like Daniel had drawn in wider audiences. The song's piano rolls were reminiscent of his heroes Jerry Lee Lewis and Little Richard, while the pounding beat and strumming guitar contain shades of The Who and The Rolling Stones. Despite its attempts to convey wildness and abandonment, the recorded version was nowhere near as animated as it was on stage. In the mid-1970s Saturday Night's Alright For Fighting was a major crowd-pleaser.

Goodbye Yellow Brick Road

Recorded: May 1973, Strawberry Studios, Château d'Hierouville, France
First released: c/w Screw You, September 1973

THE CLASSIC GOODBYE YELLOW BRICK ROAD album cover painting by Ian Beck has Elton turning his back on city life. He steps surreally through a poster stuck on a derelict wall, on which are etched a plane and a factory whose chimneys are spewing smoke, representing both the glamour and grime of urban existence. The yellow brick road winds away through hilly pastures where a bluebird flies overhead to a golden sun on the horizon.

Elton's melody conveys the paradox within Bernie's lyrics: the yellow brick road leads you where you think you want to be, but instead of finding salvation at the end, you find only disillusionment instead. The Goodbye Yellow Brick Road theme can be heard briefly at the start of the album in David Hentschel's stirring fanfare for the opening track, Funeral For A Friend (Love Lies Bleeding). A simple piano phrase opens the main version. Sweeping strings arranged by the newly recruited Del Newman gives the chorus an epic and, perversely, romantic feel. Elton's delivery is wistful, though when performed live it is more likely to generate a warm glow than pathos among the audience.

Goodbye Yellow Brick Road is the dark flipside to Follow The Yellow Brick Road, the irrepressibly cheery song from the 1939 movie The Wizard Of Oz. In the movie, Judy Garland's Dorothy has been transported by a tornado from Kansas to Munchkinland. She has to follow the yellow brick road to the Emerald City, where she will find the Wizard who she must ask to help her get home. Bernie has been to the Emerald City and yearns to return to the countryside. The yellow brick road led him from Lincolnshire to London and up various paths. Likewise with Elton, whose yellow brick road took him from being a shy, tubby schoolboy in grey flannel to the biggest selling pop star in the world with fluctuating weight, outrageous costumes and trademark spectacles.

By the time the song was written, Bernie was more likely to see himself on a ranch in California, than returning to a farm in Lincolnshire, though he had spent the first part of his marriage in a cottage in his home county. In his lyrics, the road of excess that leads to the palace of wisdom is paved with a penthouse, planes and vodka and tonics. It is a song that takes aim at the superficial world he and Elton

Goodbye Yellow Brick Road

felt ambivalent towards, though ultimately revelled in.

It is doubtful whether Bernie or Elton were trying to convey a covert meaning through the song, though Elton was always 'a friend of Dorothy' – a euphemism for being gay, inspired by Judy Garland. It was to be a couple of years before Elton publicly admitted to being 'bisexual'.

Elton was wary of releasing Goodbye Yellow Brick Road as a double album, fearing it would be too expensive for fans and suggesting simultaneous single albums instead. He was dissuaded from this because it would have been even more expensive. The double album still went to number one on both sides of the Atlantic, and stayed in both charts for nearly two years. He was sure he could have had hits with more than the four singles taken off it, but did not believe in milking an album for all it was worth.

Goodbye Yellow Brick Road is consistently voted in album polls as Elton John's best work, though he does not judge it his high point as a musician. The album may not have been held in such public esteem had it been called Vodka and Tonic, Elton's original suggestion for the title. EJ

Candle In The Wind

Recorded: May 1973, Strawberry Studios, Château d'Hierouville, France
First released: c/w Bennie and the Jets, February 1974

EVEN BEFORE IT WAS RECORDED BERNIE THOUGHT Candle In The Wind was the
best thing he and Elton had written. Bernie had been ruminating on the theme
of Marilyn Monroe since Madman Across The Water, but had never found a way
to write about her tastefully. He admitted the direct pinch from Clive Davis,
founder of Arista Records, who said the ill-starred Janis Joplin's life was like a
candle in the wind. But Davis himself had adapted the phrase from *Rolling Stone*
writer Ralph J. Gleason, whose obituary of Joplin bore the heading Another
Candle Blown Out. Gleason quoted a poem by Edna St. Vincent Millay.

  My candle burns at both ends;
  It will not last the night;
  But, ah, my foes and, oh, my friends,
  It gives a lovely light.

Gleason wrote, 'God knows, that blazing candle did cast a lovely light, even
though from time to time it flickered and the light dimmed, and the looming
face of tragedy appeared'. Bernie was also aware of the Solzhenitsyn play
entitled *Candle In The Wind.*.

The song is close to Bernie's heart, even though he was defensive about it
being received as over-sentimental. In the lyrics, he tried to convey his belief that
people fell for Marilyn not because she was a sex object, but because they saw

Candle In The Wind

her vulnerability and wanted to comfort and protect her. It is a common enough male fantasy. The fact that she is stunningly attractive helps, of course, even if you like to tell yourself you are as interested in her inner self.

As time went on, Bernie's explanations for the song's meaning grew more elaborate. In the book *Two Rooms*, published in 1991, he states, 'It's a song about media abuse. How we abuse the living, how we abuse the dead. I'm not saying she wasn't talented, but sometimes it pays to die – that's what that song's about.' As such it could refer to any media star who died prematurely (he cited James Dean as one other example). This is perhaps why the song was so aptly reincarnated in 1997 after the death of Diana, Princess of Wales.

The tone of Bernie's lyrics is bitter. According to him Marilyn was surrounded by creepy-crawlers who made her change her simple name of Norma Jean to one more publicly acceptable. The metaphor of cheapening herself in order to satisfy the lusts, sexual and financial, of those around her has more resonance. And in the light of more recent revelations over her relationship with Bobby and John F. Kennedy, more pertinence. Bernie perpetrates the stereotypical image of her, has a dig at the Hollywood machine and 'hounding' press whose influence has, if anything, become more pernicious. But however strong his sense of injustice, he manages to diffuse any pomposity by owning up to her being a childhood fantasy figure – even if she wasn't an obsession as the fans who sent him memorabilia might have thought.

Candle In The Wind did not call for any special arrangements and, though strings were discussed, they never materialised. Elton's simple four-bar piano introduction leads straight to the rather sombre main musical theme, which eschews embellishments and trills. Accompanied in the first verse by bass and drums, the guitar joins in during the first chorus playing extended notes that obviate the need for strings, while Nigel Olsson's disciplined drumming gives the whole structure backbone. The group join in on choral backing vocals as Elton's understated lower register vocals give authority and emotional uplift.

Marilyn Monroe's status has never diminished, but Bernie tired of the way she invaded his life. Elton kicked off Bernie's memorabilia collection by buying him the dress bust on which Marilyn had her dresses made, housed in a Perspex case surrounded by flashing lights. That was for his 21st birthday, which pre-dated the song by a couple of years. Bernie has kept the bust but cast the rest of his collection to the wind. 🎹

Bennie and The Jets

Bennie And The Jets

Recorded: May 1973, Strawberry Studios, Château d'Hierouville, France
First released: c/w Candle In The Wind, February 1974

A PIANO CHORD STRIKES UP only to die away quickly over the murmur of an expectant crowd. There's a brief pause before it strikes again, then again, as semi-quavers follow pauses of equal length. Bennie And The Jets is under way. The first chord was a slip which Gus Dudgeon had intended to delete when mixing the track. A careful listen at this point can detect a not entirely clean break, as Dudgeon muted the spoken count-in but left the chord. When he realised his mistake, it occurred to Dudgeon that the recalcitrant chord was what a pianist might play to a live band to signify they were about to start. It was reprieved.

To enhance the 'live' effect, Dudgeon dug out a recording of Elton at the Royal Festival Hall from February 1972 and used a snippet of audience noise from the end of a song. For the ambience during the track, he made a tape-loop of the general hubbub at the start of the same show. Dudgeon augmented this with people in the studio, himself included, who clapped, whistled and shouted, making sure it all missed the beat as English audiences often do.

Elton liked the effect though he was always under the misapprehension that Dudgeon had by chance found applause from one number which inexplicably matched another. For the close of the song, Dudgeon used a recording of a Jimi Hendrix audience which he had first put on Rock And Roll Madonna, a single from back in June 1970. In the years immediately following the release of Bennie And The Jets, Dudgeon was amused to find life imitating art as audiences clapped and whistled on cue to match the recording.

Bennie And The Jets was about a futuristic rock 'n' roll band. Bennie was a butch but beautiful girl, said to have been named after a girlfriend of Bernie's named Sally Bennington. Bennie's backing band were identical boys. Artist David Larkham was instructed on how Bernie wanted the track depicted on the album sleeve. Years later when Bernie saw the celebrated video of the Robert Palmer single Addicted To Love, directed by Terence Donovan, he thought that here was the real Bennie And The Jets, despite the gender reversal.

Bernie admitted it was a throwaway lyric of little significance. With its references to walls of sound and fighting on the street, it sounds as if he meant it to be a rock 'n' roll track. But Elton made it an upbeat slice of electric funk. He never saw it as a hit, and refused an initial request from his American record company to release it as a single. He soon relented when he learned it was an airplay hit at black stations in Detroit. He was too big a fan of black music not to enjoy the ego boost of cracking that market.

Bennie And The Jets not only topped the prestigious *Billboard* magazine Rhythm And Blues chart, a first for Elton, but crossed over and made number one in the US pop charts. In Britain it was B-side to Candle In The Wind. Two and a half years later, it was released as an A-side by DJM Records after Elton had left the label, where it reached number thirty seven. EJ

Don't Let The Sun Go Down On Me

Don't Let The Sun Go Down On Me

Recorded: January 1974, Caribou Ranch, Colorado, USA
First released: c/w Sick City, May 1974

DON'T LET THE SUN GO DOWN ON ME draws its emotional power and a feeling of foreboding from the traumas Elton was going through at the time of recording. The lyrics were apt, with their talk of growing tired and frustrated, of needing love to heal the wounds. Recording the song was far from straightforward. Elton's mental state was deteriorating. He was drinking half a bottle of scotch a day, had started his descent into cocaine hell, put on over three stone and looked and felt like a zombie. At the age of only twenty six he was conscious that his body was falling apart and his hair was disappearing fast.

The Caribou Ranch in the Rocky Mountains of Colorado promised calm vistas and pure air to help restore the jaded star. But he was in no mood to appreciate the scenery. Caribou was run by a man whose reputation Elton respected. Jimmy Guercio was manager and producer of the technically sharp brass rock band Chicago. Guercio also played bass with The Beach Boys.

Caribou was also where the song Rocky Mountain Way had been recorded by Joe Walsh. A recent hit single, it had throbbing guitar lines and vocals which sounded as if they were shouted through a megaphone. It was pointed out to Elton, after he arrived, that the sound he so admired on Walsh's record was actually created when it was re-recorded and mixed at studios in Los Angeles.

Elton should have been basking in the reception of Goodbye Yellow Brick Road and such triumphs as his Hollywood Bowl concert in September 1973, a kitsch extravaganza with celebrity lookalikes, where hundreds of white doves were released into the air from raised piano lids emblazoned with the name Elton. Instead he was worn out. He felt as if he'd been touring solidly for four and a half years.

With barely a break following Christmas dates in Britain, he flew to Denver to start recording his first studio album in the country that had given him so much inspiration. His schedule and frame of mind had allowed his stock of songs to be depleted again and most numbers were written in the first two days of his stay at Caribou.

There were unforeseen technical problems. Producer Gus Dudgeon was unfamiliar with the mixing desk and, in the thinner air 8,500 feet up, found the studio monitors reacting in an unexpected way. It took two precious days to get the sound he was after. When he'd finished, the songs were ready, but Elton was not, having slumped into one of his ever more frequent 'moods'.

The studio had only been booked for ten days, the estimated average recording time for an Elton album. Afterwards, they were due to tour Japan, Australia and New Zealand. With the limited time left, two backing tracks were recorded on one day followed by twelve songs recorded over the following three. Don't Let The Sun... was the most satisfying result from a cobbled-together album that was as inferior as Goodbye Yellow Brick Road was superior.

The chorus to Don't Let The Sun... lent itself to an epic treatment. The call went out to fly in top calibre backing singers: Dusty Springfield, whom Elton had always admired and first met at his debut appearance on *Top Of The Pops* as a star for Border Song; Danny Hutton from Three Dog Night, the first important act to cover a Taupin-John song; the trio America; and Billy Preston, best known for his keyboard playing with The Beatles. It was an ill-matched and fussy combination and Dudgeon decided to start again, bringing in some of Elton's pals from The Beach Boys. Along came Bruce Johnston (who was dating a girl who ran John Reid's office in Los Angeles), and Carl Wilson. They were accompanied by Billy Hensche, Daryl Dragon and Toni Tennille who, like Guercio, were part of the Beach Boys backing band. Daryl and Toni were better known as the successful pop harmonies duo Captain and Tennille. The vocals of Don't Let The Sun... were arranged by Johnston aided by the Captain and recorded once Elton had finished recording his vocals.

Elton and Dudgeon started rowing in the studio, something they had never done before. Elton hated his vocals and hated himself. He told Dudgeon to send it all to Engelbert Humperdinck, and if he didn't like it he could give it to Lulu. He threatened to shoot Dudgeon if he put the vocals on the album. Elton was amused to later learn he had been nominated for a Grammy Award for the Best Vocal Performance.

His fears that he would have to re-record all the vocals on Caribou subsided

when, after more detached listening, he realised that he had been over-reacting.

The next few months were ones of unrelenting stress. John Reid was arrested and spent three weeks in prison in New Zealand for assault following a row at a press reception. Elton appeared in the dock also charged with assault, though he was acquitted. Suffering from exhaustion in April and May 1974, Elton was forced to cancel his European tour. Though he did keep a date for a benefit concert at Watford Football Stadium, where he appeared with Rod Stewart prior to the release of Don't Let The Sun Go Down On Me.

Elton had first played Rod his new single as he was driving them into London from his Windsor home. Rod, terrified at Elton's speeding, remarked after listening to the song for thirty seconds, 'Slow one, is it?'

The single became Elton's fourth million-seller in America in eighteen months, reaching number two in the charts, though in Britain it only reached number sixteen. The album Caribou was a massive hit in the United States. In Britain it hit number one for two weeks and then made a rapid descent. Don't Let The Sun Go Down On Me continued to exert its influence over Elton and in times of emotional stress he could find himself choking back the words during its performance. EU

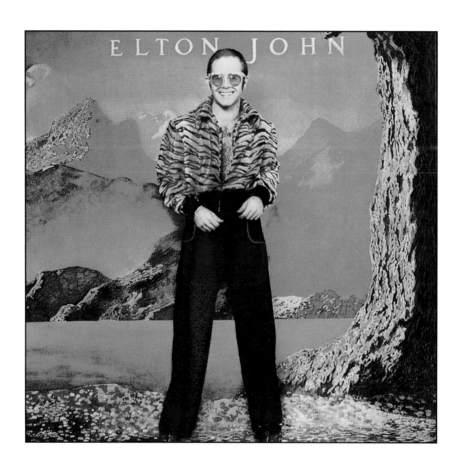

Solar Prestige A Gammon
Recorded: January 1974, Caribou Ranch, Colorado, USA
First released: Caribou album, June 1974

THE SONG'S SECRET IS IN THE TITLE. Gammon, another word for ham. Elton was always a bit of one and here he got his chance to be Kenneth Williams and Beryl Reid, Bluebottle of *The Goon Show* and a Neapolitan ice-cream vendor rolled into one.

Elton's inspiration came from the so-called Long Medley at the end of The

Solar Prestige A Gammon

Beatles' Abbey Road album. It was that 'medley with a nonsense Italian thing', as he called it, which inspired him to sing in (what he considered) an Italian accent. Why did Bernie Taupin write such purposefully meaningless and obscure lyrics? The theme was requested by Elton, fed up with fans who had nutty notions about what the words to his songs meant. But Bernie's attempt to write absolute rubbish backfired. Fans thought there was enormous significance and meaning in the song, and saw it as their job to unravel every line.

Bernie writes of 'turbert', 'salmon', 'hair ring', 'sardin' and 'cod'. Partially misspelt references, one theory goes, to the five loaves and five fishes that Jesus imparted to the faithful. It is a view that could easily flounder since there is a 'floundin' in there, too, and there are no loaves.

The history of misinterpreting Bernie's lyrics is long. On Border Song he was accused of being anti-Semitic because of 'Holy Moses'. Levon from Madman Across The Water had a son named Jesus. This was meant to be significant, as was the fact that he was a cartoon balloon salesman. Some were convinced the title Madman referred to President Richard Nixon – a good guess but wrong. There were the Daniel theories. Grey Seal from the Empty Sky album, re-recorded for Goodbye Yellow Brick Road, is impenetrable, as is Take Me To The Pilot. All enabled the theorists to get in a spin. Unless you believe that mysterious forces were using Bernie Taupin as a channel to send messages to the world, these lyrics are best regarded as the twaddle and harmless wordplay that Bernie intended them to be.

If such songs show us anything, it is Elton's astonishing capacity to turn any words, deep or nonsensical, with or without scansion, brimming with syllables and potential melismas, into melodies that make sense. However, not everyone approved of Elton's comic turn and Bernie's jape. Gus Dudgeon thought it was a piece of crap.

Pinball Wizard

Recorded: April 1974, Ramport Studio, Battersea, London
First released: c/w Harmony, March 1976

BEING A WELL BROUGHT UP YOUNG MAN, Elton always tried to be conscientious about repaying a debt. He remembered Pete Townshend's kindness in the early days of his career, such as the time Elton was second on the bill to The Who at a charity concert at the Roundhouse in London in December 1971. Townshend dedicated the evening's performance of the rock opera *Tommy* to Elton, then a one-hit rising star. A couple of years later, when Elton was by far the bigger star, Townshend approached Elton to appear in *Tommy* the movie. But Elton was not going to put pleasing Townshend above helping his own image and declined the offer of a substantial role. Townshend had offered Elton's mate Rod Stewart the small part of Pinball Wizard. Elton's advice to Rod was, 'I wouldn't touch it with a barge pole.'

About a year later, Townshend was still having trouble finding a suitable Pinball Wizard and approached Elton again. Regarding the song as the best from the rock opera, and something he would enjoy singing that was not time-consuming, Elton accepted, ignoring his own advice to Rod Stewart – who was understandably irritated at the news.

Elton was required to be in Southsea and Portsmouth for three days of filming under the direction of the mercurial Ken Russell. The two got on well. Despite rising at 5 a.m. Elton enjoyed the experience – and that of dressing as a skinhead. He had to wear terrifyingly giant Doc Marten boots attached by callipers, which allowed him to move as if on stilts. He kept the boots as mementoes and had the grace and modesty not to follow other rock stars into a movie career.

Townshend originally stipulated that he produce Elton's version of Pinball Wizard. But he later relented and acted as supervisor, while Gus Dudgeon took the controls at The Who's Ramport Studio, a converted church hall in south London. The session was completed in a day, with Elton using his own band. His version stays close to The Who's original, with a slightly extended guitar solo to synchronise with the footage and a final section lifted from The Who's first hit I Can't Explain. Townshend told Dudgeon he thought it was the best thing on the soundtrack album. Elton's track received the most airplay when the film was promoted in America, though it didn't make a single there. However, it did reach number ten in Britain when it was released as a single in 1976.

Pinball Wizard

Lucy In The Sky With Diamonds

Recorded: July 1974, Caribou Ranch, Colorado, USA
First released: c/w One Day At A Time, November 1974

THE BEATLES WERE ALWAYS THE BENCHMARK
Elton John set for himself as a fan and fellow musician. His first tenuous contact with their world was at Dick James Music. As their publisher, James would receive demo tapes of The Beatles' recordings. After his arrival at the organisation in 1967, Elton somehow managed to 'borrow' the tapes and take them home for a listen, and would hear special recordings made for fans.

John Lennon had paid Elton the greatest of compliments when he said that Your Song was the first new thing to happen since The Beatles. For Elton and Bernie, who had tried to mimic so many Beatles songs, this was manna from God himself.

Elton first became acquainted with Lennon in October 1973 through their mutual friend Tony King, who had helped out on production duties at Abbey Road during the Beatles' sessions and later ran Apple Records in America. He knew Elton through having produced an ad hoc group called The Bread and Beer Band, recording kitsch versions of well-known

Lucy In The Sky With Diamonds

tunes at Abbey Road as a laugh in 1968 and 1969. At the time of Elton's meeting with Lennon, King was executive vice president of Rocket Records.

Elton and Lennon became warm friends after Elton overcame his shyness and hero worship. It was the year of Lennon's Lost Weekend when, parted from Yoko Ono, he caroused with Harry Nilsson and lived with May Pang. He was recording his album Walls And Bridges and got stuck three-quarters of the way through the raucous rocker Whatever Gets You Thru The Night. Elton popped in on the sessions at the Record Plant in New York and offered his services singing and playing piano. Lennon eagerly accepted and Elton became a temporary member of The Plastic Ono Nuclear Band. After his contribution, Elton mentioned to Tony King that if Whatever Gets You Thru The Night reached number one, he would like Lennon to appear on stage with him to return the favour. Lennon agreed, never imagining it was a possibility as his solo record sales had recently been poor.

Elton was to ask another favour. Bernie, while viewing the cartoon Beatles movie *Yellow Submarine*, wondered why The Beatles had never released Lucy In The Sky With Diamonds as a single and suggested Elton record it. Elton was enthusiastic and, again too shy to make a direct approach, asked King if Lennon would honour him at least with his presence at the recording session even if he did not want to play.

The song was recorded during the sessions for Captain Fantastic And The Brown Dirt Cowboy, at Caribou Ranch in Colorado. As Lennon came through the control room door for the first time, Dudgeon was so awe-struck he was sure he could see Lennon's charisma manifested as a glow of light. Lennon was evidently enjoying himself, despite an asthma attack caused by the high altitude, and there was no obvious 'I'm the bigger star' style rivalry. Lennon contributed backing vocals and reggae guitar on Lucy and was credited on the record as 'Dr Winston O'Boogie & His Reggae Guitars'. He also contributed to Elton's version of his recent composition One Day At A Time. The combined power of their names proved irresistible and Lucy reached number ten in the UK and number one in the USA.

Elton performs a reasonable Lennon impersonation on the song. Less psychedelic and more rhythmic, his version has a dance feel which The

Lucy In The Sky With Diamonds

Beatles' version certainly lacked. Lennon's voice is barely discernible though his reggae guitar does give the chorus a catchy swing.

With Whatever Ever Gets You Thru The Night having already reached number one, Lennon knew he would have to honour his word about appearing on stage. Before committing himself he went to see Elton perform in Boston and got stage fright backstage just watching him prepare. Lennon did finally agree to appear with Elton however, at his 1974 Thanksgiving Day concert at Madison Square Garden, New York.

At the rehearsal Elton said he wanted Lennon to perform Imagine but the former Beatle refused, saying he did not want to come on like Dean Martin and play his classic hits. He said he wanted to have fun and play some rock 'n' roll and would do no more than three numbers because it was Elton's show. Backstage, Lennon received a gardenia and a good luck message from Yoko, his still estranged wife. He was relieved, believing that she was not in the audience as his stage fright would have been too much to bear. However, Elton knew Yoko was actually there.

Lennon threw up before going on stage and was too nervous to tune his guitar, asking Davey Johnstone to do it for him. He tried to get Bernie to go on with him, eventually managing it on his own to storming applause which lasted over ten minutes and left Elton and the band in tears at the emotion in the hall. The friends performed Whatever Gets You Thru The Night, Lucy In The Sky With Diamonds and I Saw Her Standing There. Lennon was surprised to see Yoko backstage and it marked the resumption of their relationship. Elton's role as friend was acknowledged when he became godfather to their son, Sean.

The Madison Square Garden show was to be Lennon's last live concert appearance. Elton marked Lennon's death with an instrumental, The Man Who Never Died. Writing it proved a cathartic exercise. The song made it as a B-side, but it was Empty Garden (Hey Hey Johnny), released on the 1982 album Jump Up!, that served as his and Bernie's official tribute. Bernie, who was also close to Lennon, locked himself in his room the day after Lennon's death and wrote the angry words which Elton recorded, conveying their shared feeling of senseless loss, confusion and affection. 🎹

We All Fall In Love Sometimes

Written by: Elton John, Bernie Taupin
Recorded: June to August 1974, Caribou Ranch, Colorado
First released: Captain Fantastic And The Brown Dirt Cowboy album, May 1975

THEIRS WAS A PLATONIC LOVE, unconditional and pure. One was the brother the other had always wanted. Both became the closest friends they would ever find, bound together as soul mates and workmates.

We All Fall In Love Sometimes is a courageously honest account of the formation of Elton and Bernie's intimate, innocent relationship and their struggle to write great songs. We All Fall In Love Sometimes still means more to Elton than anything else he and Bernie wrote together.

Bernie's sleight of hand is to make it appear that he is writing about two young lovers rather than he and Elton; there are 'heavy eyes', 'starlight' and a 'full moon'. He refers directly to the Empty Sky album and a time 'filled with laughter', before innocence was swamped by success.

The harpsichord on We All Fall... echoes Elton's use of the same instrument on Skyline Pigeon, and there is a similar sense of wistfulness and yearning in the melody. The Mellotron and ARP synthesizer create a rich orchestral effect. Davey Johnstone's restrained acoustic and electric guitars and the backing band's vocal harmonies contribute to the masterful climax as the song moves from mellow reflection to stirring resolve.

We All Fall In Love Sometimes segues into Curtains, the final track on the Captain Fantastic album, which continues with the same tempo and a similar melody. Curtains alludes to their earliest songs and ends with the inference that we can all make our dreams come true.

Unlike anything Elton and Bernie had written before, Captain Fantastic And The Brown Dirt Cowboy was carefully planned and written in sequence, the writers consulting each other on the order and themes. After the slapdash Caribou they had to do something to restore their credibility.

The idea for the album germinated with Dogs In The Kitchen, Bernie's bitterly cynical portrayal of corporate greed in the entertainment industry. It was not, it seems, referring to Dick James but to a familiar world, nevertheless.

Bernie cannot remember where the names 'Captain Fantastic' and 'the Brown

We All Fall In Love Sometimes

Dirt Cowboy' came from, though they could be leftover from their original idea to make - horror of horrors - a science-fiction concept album.

Elton was hesitant at first, self-conscious that writing about himself would be seen as conceited, even if he was his own favourite subject. Both promised each other they would add comical touches to defuse any pomposity, though the only apparent humour is in the packaging. For this, Bernie approached artist Alan Aldridge, a leading Seventies pop artist, known for his *The Butterfly Ball* painting. His fantastical cover memorably depicts Elton as the Mad Hatter in an eye mask riding his piano like a horse, atop a swarm of smiling and clothed animals. Bernie is cooped up in a floating glass bubble.

Elton wrote most of the melodies to Captain Fantastic on the final trip of the liner S.S. *France*, from Southampton to New York, on his way to record in Colorado. He would squeeze into the music room for two hours each day while an opera singer who had prior claim to the room took her lunch break.

The Dogs In The Kitchen lyric is printed on the cover, although the tune does not actually feature, having been deemed musically unsuitable. The first tune is the title track, an affectionate reminiscence on the backgrounds of the two unlikely heroes from genteel suburbia and country idyll, too full of talent, ambition and determination to be content with their lot. What follows is the tale of their career: Tower Of Babel is their first meeting; Bitter Fingers, their first attempts to write hits; Tell Me When The Whistle Blows refers to Bernie's homesickness; (Gotta Get A) Meal Ticket, to signing their first contract; Better Off Dead, seeking inspiration; Writing, their art.

Despite the problems encountered on Caribou they returned to the Caribou Ranch for Captain Fantastic. Gus Dudgeon overcame the technical problems this time aided by house engineers. All songs were rehearsed and recorded in running order, likewise overdubbed and mixed, allowing the sound and feel of the album to flow more gracefully than normal. It took an unprecedented month to record, while mixing took Dudgeon a further two months. Captain Fantastic And The Brown Dirt Cowboy became the first album to enter the American Billboard chart at number one where it stayed for seven weeks. In Britain it reached number two after four previous number ones that included the Greatest Hits album of November 1974. Captain Fantastic And The Brown Dirt Cowboy marked a creative peak which Elton and Bernie would never consistently reach again. ▣

Someone Saved My Life Tonight

Someone Saved My Life Tonight

Written by: Elton John, Bernie Taupin
Recorded: June to August 1974, Caribou Ranch, Colorado
First released: c/w House of Cards, June 1975

IN THE DAYS BEFORE GAY LIBERATION fully asserted itself there were still plenty of homosexual men who, failing to acknowledge their true tendencies, got married and fathered children. Elton John was about to join their ranks, just three weeks away from matrimony. The cake was made. He had chosen the soft furnishings and the drapes, which in itself should have been a warning signal to him.

His bride-to-be was Linda Woodrow, four years his senior and somewhat taller at six feet, heiress to the family that owned Epicure pickles. The couple met on Christmas Eve 1967 at a cabaret club in Sheffield when Elton was in Long John Baldry's backing band. He felt for Linda's sorry tale of a midget boyfriend who drove around in a specially adapted Mini and beat her up. After following him to another gig the next week he found himself desperately in love and invited her to live with him in London.

They found a basement in a grimy corner of Islington in North London where Bernie became their flatmate. Newly contracted to Dick James Music, the fledgling songwriters fell prey to domestic altercations which hampered their concentration. Linda disapproved of her fiancé's chosen career and his music (she was a fan of balladeer Mel Tormé), pressing him to get a more stable job. Later Elton would claim that Linda's attempts to persuade him got physical.

It was nine months of hell for Elton who came close to a nervous breakdown before attempting what he called a 'Woody Allen style' suicide by resting his head on a cushion placed in the oven, turning the gas on low and leaving the windows open. Linda could not understand how he could waste all that gas.

As the wedding loomed Elton and Bernie, on a night out, bumped into Long John Baldry at the Bag O' Nails club in Soho. Baldry cautioned Elton that he must be mad and surely was not in love with Linda. How, Baldry wondered, could she love him when she beat him up and smashed him in the face?

More pertinently, Baldry was gay himself and recognised it in Elton, warning him his sexuality would destroy him if he did not come to terms with it. Elton had not even suspected Baldry was gay. Getting drunker and drunker they all staggered out and Elton pledged, 'It's over, it's finished.' He broke the badly received news to Linda that night and the next day he and Bernie were safely back in Northwood Hills.

Elton was sued for breach of promise and Linda won damages. He thereafter lived in fear she would one day turn up. Tracked down in the early Nineties by tabloid newspapers, Linda disputed many of his allegations and in a swipe back proclaimed he was a lousy and infrequent lover.

Bernie has stated that Someone Saved My Life Tonight was about the suicide attempt and the marriage that never was. Elton has a different emphasis, saying it had nothing to do with him putting his head in the oven and was actually about Long John Baldry and his own troublesome sexuality. Baldry is the 'sugar bear' of the song. 'Baldry saved my fucking life in every sense of that phrase', Elton told Mojo magazine in October 1997.

Bernie's lyrics are explicit. The whole incident is there, Linda is the 'prima donna' whose hooks nearly dragged Elton to the altar, the 'pawn' outplayed by 'a dominating queen'. It describes how, at four in the morning, Elton told her he would be sleeping alone that night. There's a reference to her inheritance of 'stocks and bonds' and how Elton avoided a nine-to-five fate. His stepdad's truck (in reality a Ford Cortina) even makes an appearance, taking him (and Bernie) home to mum.

Elton pays musical tribute to Brian Wilson's genius as an arranger, to Carl Wilson's sweet voice and to the underrated 1972 Beach Boys album Carl And The Passions: So Tough, for influencing this track. The sound of the Beach Boys had, by this time, become more sombre and their arrangements simpler.

Elton's piano introduction to the song is dramatic and portentous. He enunciates the opening lines clearly as he sets the scene, his voice rising to the chorus with its California style vocal harmonies. As the story unfolds, so Elton's piano pounding becomes more dramatic and his voice more cutting. He softens for the chorus as he sings the title line and his saviour comes to mind. The final repetition of Someone Saved My Life Tonight becomes a chant in celebration of his freedom as the song fades out to a celebratory vocal chorus. Undoubtedly a masterpiece.

Sorry Seems To Be The Hardest Word

Sorry Seems To Be The Hardest Word
Written by: Elton John, Bernie Taupin
Recorded: March 1976, Eastern Sound, Toronto
First released: c/w Shoulder Holster, October 1976

THE PURCHASE OF A MANSION in Beverly Hills in late 1975 was designed to give Elton a stable base in America, a haven to calm his state of mind and ease the taxman's claim on his wallet. Instead the L.A. lifestyle left him a druggier and boozier wreck. To this was added a fear for his safety when he woke one day to find a girl fan at the edge of his bed.

Bernie was already a resident of Los Angeles having long since abandoned his snug cottage, Piglet-in-the-Wilds in Lincolnshire, where he spent the first year after he wed Maxine. He too was going through emotional upheaval coping with his marriage separation and alcoholism. Bernie was visiting Elton one day and heard him etch out a melody line on the piano. This time they broke their convention of not writing in the same room, albeit momentarily, and the line 'Sorry seems to be the hardest word' crystallised in Bernie's mind. The title to the song, always the starting point for Bernie, summed up the brooding self-pity and regret felt by both lyricist and melodist.

A final plea to Maxine from Bernie, Sorry... was tinged with both hopelessness and panic. The sheet music bears the instruction 'slow lament'. The recording has strings and accordion for extra desolation.

Sorry... appears on the Blue Moves album with other songs so downbeat they almost grind into the ground. Someone's Final Song is about a suicidal songwriter; Between Seventeen and Twenty referred to Maxine and Bernie's ages when they married and her betrayal. For extra tragedy there is an Edith Piaf tribute Cage The Songbird; Idol is about the downfall of Elvis and a prediction of the future for Elton. Finally, there's the self-explanatory If There's a God in Heaven (What's He Waiting For?).

The song titles were a presage of the atmosphere during the recording of the album in Toronto, which took place over three weeks in March and April 1976. Elton's usual punctuality deserted him. At times he would show up and not want to play, and sat in the studio sulking. Davey Johnstone and Ray Cooper, the musicians closest to him, were in charge of bringing him round.

Gone were Dee Murray and Nigel Olsson and in their place was the band hired for the previous (poor) Rock Of The Westies album, including old chum Caleb Quaye on guitar who added more of a rock feel, and keyboard player James Newton Howard, later to become one of Hollywood's leading movie soundtrack composers, to allow Elton more flexibility on stage. Newton Howard arranged the strings on Sorry Seems To Be The Hardest Word.

Overcome by the failure of a miserable love affair Elton had tried to commit suicide again while on the Rock Of The Westies tour in autumn 1975. He had flown his family over to be with him in Los Angeles. They were surprised to see him throw himself in the hotel swimming pool screaming, 'I'll be dead in two hours', after swallowing 80-odd Valium tablets. His unfazed grandmother Ivy deadpanned, 'Oh, I suppose we'd better go home now.' Within days he was unveiling his star on Hollywood Boulevard and performing two ecstatically-received nights at the Dodgers Stadium dressed in a sequinned baseball uniform.

Blue Moves was the first Elton John album released on his new Rocket Records label in Britain. Intended as a single album called Black Moves it became a double on the insistence of MCA Records in America where he was signed to a new groundbreaking $8 million deal.

Instead of the usual picture of Elton, the Blue Moves cover was a painting by Patrick Procktor called *The Guardian Readers*. The all-male group of picnickers was a curiously homosexual scene for the closet homosexual pop star. Though not as artistically dire as Rock Of The Westies, Blue Moves marked the start of a decline in record sales for Elton. Breaking the line of seven number ones in America it reached number three, sharing the same position in Britain.

The single of Sorry Seems To Be the Hardest Word sold a million copies in America though in the UK it failed to reach the top ten. This cannot have been helped by DJM, his old company, releasing Bennie And The Jets as a single a month before which failed to make the top thirty. The release of Sorry... coincided with Elton announcing at the end of 1976 that he was coming off the road, mentally and physically exhausted. [EJ]

Don't Go Breaking My Heart

Written by: Ann Orson, Carte Blanche
Recorded: April 1976, Eastern Sound, Toronto and Marquee Studios, London
First released: c/w Snow Queen, June 1976

KIKI DEE WAS THE FIRST EUROPEAN signing to Motown Records. When its label boss John Reid left to manage Elton John she maintained contact. As her career with Motown fizzled out Reid brought her to Elton's notice and signed her to Rocket Records. Despite accidentally smashing house-proud Elton's champagne glasses at his flat on their first meeting, a strong bond developed. They were born just nineteen days apart, both well brought up and well behaved children from humble roots (she was born Pauline Matthews from Bradford). Both grew up R&B fans. Elton guided her to two Top 20 hits on Rocket before the idea for a duet grew out of an American tour in 1974, during which Kiki was the opening act. They had often talked admiringly of Tammi Terrell and Marvin Gaye's sixties Motown duets and Don't Go Breaking My Heart is a tribute to that sound.

The song came to Elton as he was toying around on the Wurlitzer electric piano in the studio at the end of the Blue Moves album sessions. He asked Gus Dudgeon to listen to his latest tune. Unusually it was not based on a Bernie Taupin lyric but a title of Elton's own invention. 'Don't go breaking my heart, don't go breaking my heart...' he sang and played. Dudgeon worked out what the song was going to be called but needed another listen, preferably without the tedious repetition. Instead he got an Elton speciality, a stream of ad-libbed gobbledegook. Agreeing that the tune had potential, Dudgeon put the tape on. Armed with this Elton phoned Bernie on holiday in Barbados, ignoring the fact it was the middle of the night. He teased that he had a real test for him, to turn the line 'Don't go breaking my heart' into a duet with Kiki Dee. Bernie was happy to oblige and told Elton to send him a tape.

Don't Go Breaking My Heart

In a hurry, as ever, Elton who insisted on playing the tape over the phone.

The resulting Taupin lyrics showed a lack of thought and little heart. Maybe that's why he sanctioned the jokey pseudonyms of Anne Orson and Carte Blanche (as in horse and cart, Cockney rhyming slang for fart). Here was a mildly suggestive tale about knocking on a door and being given the key, rhyming 'down' and 'clown' and 'start' and 'heart.' Bernie did, however, break off his holiday to deliver his efforts to the studio. The only person not there was Kiki. Her vocal would have to be added later back in London. The weary musicians who thought their efforts were just about over were called back into the studio. The tune was given a disco pop arrangement helped by a funky guitar groove courtesy of Caleb Quaye and a bopping string arrangement added later by James Newton Howard.

During the recording Elton started singing all the verses. Dudgeon wanted to know if it was to be a true duet or whether Kiki was to just make a guest appearance. Alternating lines sounded like the best option with Elton opening the song. To get round Kiki's absence Elton sang the whole song while Dudgeon 'buttoned out' Kiki's part. With the master tape prepared, Elton then ghosted Kiki's lines on a demo, mimicking her in the process. All Kiki had to do back in London was follow Elton's lead parrot fashion, dutifully putting down her vocals under Dudgeon's guidance. At an earlier recording session for I Got The Music In Me, Elton had helped Kiki overcome her vocal block by streaking across the studio. Without his presence to bounce off she was now worried about not hitting the right key.

The first time Elton and Kiki sang the song together was for a video shoot in the early days of the art-form. Kiki was dressed in a jump-suit that made her look like the children's TV puppet Andy Pandy. Elton, without his piano to pound, was waving his arms around a lot. (Ten years later they would perform it in front of a billion people at Live Aid.) The single reached number one on both sides of the Atlantic in July 1976. It was Kiki's first and only pole position and the first time in five and a half years of chart success that Elton had a single top the British charts.

Elton likes to adopt causes, and Kiki was one of the women singers he chose to champion. As well as their shared roots he saw in her his own lack of self-confidence. Their personalities however were vastly different. Where she was prone to take other peoples advice, his driving sense of purpose made sure Elton John was pushed to the fore. Kiki thought she had arrived when she got to number one, not realising she should have seen it only as the beginning. 🎹

Part-Time Love

Part-Time Love
Written by: Elton John, Gary Osborne
Recorded: Between January and
September 1978, The Mill, Cookham,
Berkshire
First released: c/w I Cry at Night,
October 1978

SITTING UP IN BED WATCHING TV at his
Berkshire mansion, Elton happened
upon an interview with The Sex
Pistols, The Clash and Siouxsie and The
Banshees. They were having a go at
him and other old dinosaurs. Although
peeved at first, he would soon
applaud the kicking that punk gave to
the complacent old order of which he
was so much a part.

Throughout the second year of punk,
1977, Elton had bided his time,
playing just a few shows and
recording nothing. He was reassessing
his own life. After coming off the road
he had the wisdom to take on a
project in the real world, becoming
chairman of his much loved Watford
Football Club and trying to propel it
from ignominy near the bottom of the
Fourth Division to a team of national
standing. In the directors box he had
to put up with opposing supporters
chanting 'Don't sit down while Elton's
around or you might get a penis up
your arse,' after his recent admission

in *Rolling Stone* magazine that he was 'bisexual'.

Elton had become weary of Bernie's depressing lyrics after Blue Moves and though there never was a formal decision to break, early in 1978 he found himself teaming up with lyricist and jingles composer Gary Osborne. They had been introduced by mutual friends and Elton enjoyed Osborne's uncomplicated, jokey company. Elton was in Gus Dudgeon's new studio. The Mill in Berkshire, recording Ego, a left-over Bernie song, and Shine On Through, which he'd written with Gary.

Once in the studio, he told Radio 1 DJ Andy Peebles, he got 'writer's diarrhoea' and the A Single Man album flowed. Which is an apt description, for there was little on the new album that was edifying. However arcane Bernie's meanderings, his words at least had a knack of forcing Elton to stretch himself to match the often uneasy metres or word juxtapositions. Osborne's lyrics though, were predictable, neatly ordered in thought and verse, and invariably about the peaks and troughs of love at its most clichéd. The songwriting process was also more conventional with Gary writing the lyrics around Elton's melodies after they'd discussed what each song was about.

Part-Time Love became the first single and characterised the mundane standard of Osborne's doggerel. It is a sprightly pop tune that owed much to The Four-Tops. The lyrics at least had the diversion of being ambivalent. They seem to be saying that everyone has a bit on the side so don't worry about it. But then again it could be about an illicit love affair and while the presumably married man says it's acceptable for him to have a wife at home it is not acceptable for his mistress to take another lover. The true meaning is hardly important and was never intended to be. But the combination of jobbing music and lyrics only served to highlight how unadventurous Elton had become.

Though recorded at The Mill. A Single Man was the first album in a six year run of astounding success not to be produced by Gus Dudgeon, who had left the organisation after a row over the running of Rocket Records of

Part-Time Love

which he was A&R Director. He was still friends with Elton and would pop into the studio to listen to what his successor Clive Franks, his touring sound engineer, was achieving with Elton as co-producer. It all tinkled along but lacked Dudgeon's knack of intricate arrangements and atmospheres. Part-Time Love saw the return of Paul Buckmaster's string arrangements though here they are insipid. Gone were the new band, to be replaced by session musicians joining the stalwart Davey Johnstone and Ray Cooper.

Inside the A Single Man album cover Elton was pictured in a vintage Jaguar dressed in tweeds like a country squire. He was trying to shed the glam image, but it only served to signal how far removed he was from the do-it-yourself musical energy surging through decaying urban Britain in the wake of the Punk and New Wave movements.

On the cover he is pictured with a top hat, wearing a Watford F.C. tie, old judo trousers tucked into Cuban heeled boots and looking like an eccentric undertaker standing on the path in Windsor Great Park with Windsor Castle in the background. Gone from the bridge of his nose were the glasses he was always pushing back into place. He was wearing contact lenses in a further attempt to reinvent himself, but such a cosmetic change could not alter the often confused and unhappy individual inside.

He was sure some of his vocal performances on A Single Man were among the best of his career. It sounds more like he was going through the motions, not the emotions. Closest was the instrumental that ended the album. Composed and recorded in the same day it felt like a death song, though he could think of no title. The next day came the news that 17-year-old Rocket Records messenger boy Guy Burchett had been killed on his motorcycle. The instrumental was dedicated to him as Song For Guy.

Elton had his own death scare soon after Part-Time Love was released in October 1978. He was taken to hospital with a suspected heart attack which turned out to be a panic attack brought on by exhaustion. He ruefully looked back on the incident and noted that the song, a minor hit, at least started selling many times more when the news broke he was in hospital. EJ

Victim Of Love

Victim of Love

Written by: Pete Bellotte
Recorded: August 1979, Musicland Studios, Munich
First released: c/w Strangers, September 1979

WHAT POSSESSED ELTON JOHN TO RECORD the album Victim Of Love must be
a question he has frequently asked himself. It must have sounded quite an
appealing idea at first. His old mate Pete Bellotte would do all the work,
songwriting, arranging and producing. Elton didn't even have to touch a
keyboard. All he had to do was fly in, sing, and fly out again on the same day
and *voila*; an album.

Decisions borne of laziness and hubris rarely produce successful results and
Victim Of Love is widely regarded as Elton John's nadir. At a time when his
career was in a trough he should have been wary of quick fixes and band-
wagon jumping. There may have been some nobility in Elton's decision, wishing
to do an old mate a favour, but Bellotte had been doing alright for himself. If
Elton had felt any conviction about doing this album there would have been no
question of him handing over control to anybody.

He should have learnt the lesson of two years before when he worked with
Thom Bell, one of the architects of the lushly romantic R&B Sound of
Philadelphia that Elton so admired. Elton recorded two of his own compositions
and four chosen by Bell who provided the musicians and produced. The result
was diluted Philly. Though displeased with the mix, which was eventually
released as a mini-LP in America and an EP in Britain, Elton at least credited
Bell with helping him broaden his vocal range down the scale.

Philly led directly to disco. The Bee Gees and *Saturday Night Fever* and The
Village People had made disco the sound of 1978. Everyone had been
clambering on board the disco bus. Elton's old mate Rod Stewart had
released his self-confessed low point Do Ya Think I'm Sexy? Following some
way behind was Elton, recording this album, as he later acknowledged, when
the fad was on the wane.

Elton had been organist in Bluesology playing the Top Ten Club in Hamburg
when he first came across Pete Bellotte, who played in another group on the

same bill. They stayed in touch for a few years and then lost contact until Bellotte turned up backstage at the Drury Lane Theatre in London in April 1979. Elton was on a tour that marked his return from the retirement he had announced less than eighteen months before. Bellotte had married a German woman and moved to Munich where he became a songwriter and producer with Georgio Moroder. In the early Seventies they had brought the world Chicory Tip's execrable bubblegum effort Son Of My Father before helping Donna Summer become world disco queen, co-writing and co-producing her greatest hits Love To Love You Baby and I Feel Love.

Bellotte wondered whether his old chum fancied doing an album that fused disco and rock 'n' roll. Elton agreed, he'd always been a fan of dance music, as long as Bellotte was happy not to use any Elton John songs. The call came when Elton was in Nice writing for the album 21 at 33. He flew to Munich for eight hours to do the job which included eight minutes worth of Johnny B. Goode-goes-disco-bop, saved from ignominy by a sax solo from Lenny Pickett, and slugged it out with crass arrangements that have the breath of life sucked out of them.

At the time of the album's release Elton was unrepentant, admitting it was self-indulgent but saying he had no regrets, that he had wanted to make a record which ordinary punters felt compelled to dance to. Sadly for him this was unlikely to be the case. The result did not encourage you to get out of your seat, unless it was to smash the record against a wall unable to bear its thirty-five minutes of dross.

The title song has the merit of being catchy but Elton fails to carry it. There is too much electronic knob twiddling and flashy synthesizer whizzing between the speakers, all strangling Elton's voice. The number calls for camp histrionics but instead Elton's highly developed sense of melodrama leaves him, and he takes the victim lyrics too literally resulting in a tragic performance. 🄴🅄

Dressing The Part

Dressing The Part
As Donald Duck, Central Park, New York, 13 September, 1980.

HE HAS OFTEN BLAMED IT ON HIS FATHER, who would not let him wear anything as adventurous as Hush Puppy suede shoes. The likelihood though is that Elton had an innate tendency to dress up that would have turned out no different even if Stanley Dwight had been less strict and indulged his little lad.

His hair loss, his weight, his glasses and some of the wildest outfits known to rock define the Elton John look. Ever since his earliest publicity photographs Elton made sure he combed his hair forward. He had started prematurely thinning on top in his early twenties, and until he unveiled his weave in 1992 his battle with his bonce was a sad sight to see and for him to bear.

He soon emerged chrysalis-like from the image of the dour singer song-writer of the first Elton John album cover, competing with early Seventies glam rockers for the pottiest dress creation. Sequins and stacked platform shoes formed a big part of everything and though baldness beckoned, he made little attempt to cover it up during his first decade of celebrity.

The oversized glasses were probably his most recognizable fashion statements, hundreds and hundreds of them from big mask-like round frames to hide the face he was self-conscious about, to ones that flashed on and off, spelt out ZOOM and ELTON, featured palm trees and grand pianos, came with clouds and feathers, or were made to look like hornets eyes in honour of the mascot of Watford F.C. In the documentary *Tantrums And Tiaras* we saw his meticulously filed, colour co-ordinated collection that still goes everywhere with him.

As the costumes got wilder so Bernie Taupin would cringe more inside as he saw Elton interpret his serious songs looking like a circus act. The most extreme example saw the singer coming on as Donald Duck for a free concert in New York's Central Park in 1980. There were others; dressed as the Statue of Liberty, fluorescent cork balls attached to wires making them appear to float around his head; a bejewelled swimming hat creation with feathers sprouting from his shoulders; outsized glam punk Mohican; a turbanned Ali Pasha; bewigged as Amadeus Mozart. There was every conceivable hat from baseball and cowboy, to tam o'shanter, bowler and Nehru. It was rare to see him wear the same clothes more than once. The wide lapels and loon pants of the Seventies metamorphosed into the padded shoulders, winged collars and bow ties of the Eighties. But it was the emergence of Gianni Versace as a fashion genius that gave Elton the perfect look of well-tailored flamboyance, still allowing him to be flashy

Dressing The Part

when he needed to and conservative when that was called for, all the time catering for his expanding waistline. Another scene in *Tantrums And Tiaras* has him going through a Versace shop like a contestant from *Supermarket Sweep*. So great were his clothes purchases that he has held sales in New York and London selling off his clothes to raise hundreds of thousands of pounds for charity.

In 1977, after years of anguish he succumbed to the lure of a hair transplant, going to a Paris surgeon who grafted squares of hair from the back of his scalp on to the bald front. It was painful, expensive and futile, leaving him with pockets of hair that failed to cover the necessary acreage. For a time he let what hair he had grow long from the sides, then it would be cropped or dyed platinum. The weave was to solve the problem. Its first incarnation was in a page boy cut, a curiously anachronistic style that went out among girls in the typing pool about 15 years earlier. He was stung by critics who said it looked like he had a dead squirrel on his head. But he persisted, and the next style was pudding-basin schoolboy, finally coming to rest at its most aesthetically satisfying, an auburn fringed mop top. Having tired of wearing hats, 'I felt like Mrs Shilling at Derby Day,' he was finally happy, able to swim in his weave, wash it at home and feel like he looked 20 years younger.

The stage outfits have long since become more demure. But when he gets the chance to put on a bit of drag his old self will out. For his 50th birthday celebrations in March 1997 he dressed as a cross between Marie Antoinette and Le Roi Soleil wearing a three and a half foot wig topped with a replica silver galleon and a 35-foot-long white train of ostrich feathers borne by two Adonis-style attendants. EJ

Two Rooms At The End Of The World

Two Rooms At The End Of The World
Written by: Elton John, Bernie Taupin
Recorded: August 1979, Superbear Studios, Nice
First released: 21 at 33 album, May 1980

IT HAS BECOME A TIRESOME joke with Bernie and Elton that people still ask them when they are getting back together again. The truth is their split lasted just three years at the end of the Seventies. After Blue Moves Bernie was exhausted with fame and the lifestyle. A doctor's diagnosis that his liver was shot finally made him realise his very life depended on his getting away. In *Elton: The Definitive Biography* he told author Philip Norman how he rented a house in Acapulco overlooking the sea and fashioned his own recovery for three months.

Two Rooms At The End Of The World is a biographical sketch of Bernie and Elton's often irksome but fundamentally loving relationship. It tells how, after staying away from each other, they had inevitably made contact again. Bernie points out that being on opposite sides of the world is no measure of how close he and Elton feel. They might have fought with each other – at times on the road Bernie would tell his friend to go to hell and storm off – but they always drifted back. They had to struggle with their relationship while coming to terms with their own personalities and the whirlwind around them.

In the song Bernie writes of the rough ride they had endured, using the epic imagery of 'knights', a 'wagon', a 'dragon' and good old 'dirt roads'. He alludes to the gossip – will they/won't they get back together again/had they changed too much? He notes they are different, and the chorus concludes in rather biblical terms, where you find one, you will always find the other.

The reunion was at Elton's instigation, according to Philip Norman. In August 1979 Elton invited Bernie and his new wife Toni Russo to stay with him in Nice, where he was recording the album 21 at 33 (a tortuous reference to the 21 albums Elton had made at the age of 33, if you add doubles, compilations and live albums). Bernie wrote three songs for the album including Two Rooms. There were still other collaborators around, including Gary Osborne, Judie Tzuke (a folkie torch singer signed to Rocket), and Tom Robinson of Glad To Be Gay fame who co-wrote the catchy Never Gonna Fall In Love Again. Though the album was greeted as a return to form and was Elton's biggest success since Blue Moves, it has a patchy feel. His style had become more up tempo and poppy, his singing more abrasive. His rendition of Two Rooms is funky, with a brass arrangement and a forgettable melody. He seems out of kilter with lyrics that suggest a more emotive and reflective approach.

Elton and Bernie's creative hiatus had resulted in two sub-standard albums from Elton, while Bernie had worked with his friend, neighbour and fellow substance abuser Alice Cooper on an album renouncing their former lifestyle. With his new, clean-living mentality, Bernie wrote White Lady White Powder for 21 at 33. The irony was that its singer Elton was still using, even as he repeated Bernie's powerful images of the madness the drug induced and its fatal risks. Though the partners were reconciled, Bernie was dissatisfied with just being another songwriter. He was sure Elton and he could only do their best work when no-one else was involved. EJ

I'm Still Standing

Written by: Elton John, Bernie Taupin
Recorded: September 1982, Air Studios, Paris
First released: c/w Earn While You Learn, July 1983

THOUGH OSTENSIBLY ABOUT RECOVERING from a failed love affair, I'm Still Standing was a pertinent reminder to non-believers that Elton was not going to allow himself to be written out of the script in the early Eighties. What few knew was the extent to which he was still emotionally unstable, drinking and drugging heavily. The message however was clear, he was a survivor willing to tackle all opponents.

Elton's star had been in eclipse for the past six years, though he would always be a superstar having achieved a level of fame that was for life. The new pop of 1983 had virtually erased all memory of the punk era. It was the year of Michael Jackson's Thriller, the year glam returned with Culture Club and Duran Duran and synth-pop beep-beeped through the charts. Elton's pop genes fitted neatly into the stream of things. I'm Still Standing is an uncomplicated tune in 4/4 time that nudges inside the listener's brain and scores by virtue of almost static and annoyingly catchy repetitive notes. It became his biggest hit in Britain for over four years reaching number four while Too Low For Zero became his first top ten album in five years.

It felt a bit like old times in the Elton John camp during the recording of Too Low For Zero. All the interlopers had been elbowed out and Elton and Bernie were the only writers. Old band members Nigel Olsson and Dee Murray (back as contributors since 21 at 33 after a five-year lay off) were fully reinstated, joining Davey Johnstone to recreate the band from Elton's most successful period.

The relative newcomer was Chris Thomas for whom this was only his second Elton John album as sole producer. Thomas, an old acquaintance of Elton and fellow alumni of the Royal Academy of Music, was one of the leading producers of the early Eighties. Having assisted George Martin on late Beatles recordings he was an assistant on Pink Floyd's Dark Side of the Moon and had produced Wings and The Pretenders.

I'm Still Standing

Bernie and Elton were still rebuilding their relationship at this time and prior to recording the album on the Caribbean island of Montserrat, Elton stayed with Bernie and his wife Toni in Los Angeles. Incredibly, for the first time in their career, they talked about each other's songwriting. Elton listened as Bernie made suggestions about the music while Bernie heard Elton's criticism of his words.

Elton and Bernie's bond was based on shared endeavour and respect. Their brotherly love was contained within tightly drawn social parameters where certain topics were taboo. Like typical blokes they never discussed their inner life. Interviewed in the book *Two Rooms* Elton noted, 'We tell each other nothing. That's the problem. We know what's going on in each other's lives but it's very hard to crack us. We've never communicated really on a personal level, it's been an emotional relationship. It's very hard to describe but there are things about Bernie that I still don't know and stuff he still doesn't know about me.'

Whatever happened they always jealously guarded their relationship, and both admitted they had been envious of the people each other worked with. Too Low For Zero was their chance to prove that theirs was a special relationship no-one could match. The title song, about an insomnia sufferer unable to face the day, was a negative note to re-launch their full-time partnership. Some plodding lyrics like Whipping Boy and the melody to Crystal, worthy of a beginner's guide to the home organ, should have been booted out. Other numbers like Cold As Christmas and I Guess That's Why They Call It The Blues (co-written with Davey Johnstone) were reminiscent of their salad days.

Another song on the album, Kiss The Bride, also became a minor hit. It was an uncomplicated story of a wedding ceremony where the bride's former boyfriend wishes they were still together. Within a year the song would have a more poignant relevance being played at the wedding celebrations between Elton John and Renate Blauel. She was a humble studio engineer who first met Elton at Air Studios in London in March 1983 during the mixing sessions for Too Low For Zero. She received 'special thanks' on the album credits: it was the first anyone in the wider world knew of her existence. EJ

Marriage to Renate Blauel
14 February, 1984

RENATE BLAUEL SUCCUMBED to a not uncommon feminine delusion, that she could somehow convert a gay man into becoming straight. Elton, his mind fogged on drugs and alcohol, thought marriage was the antidote to the unhappiness he had experienced in gay relationships.

Of all the people who came into the circle of fire around Elton, Renate is the one whose dignity he has repeatedly expressed admiration for, as well as regret at the unhappiness he caused her. Renate was the coy daughter of middle class German parents. Before meeting Elton she lived a simple existence in a humble flat in North West London. She had hoped to become a record producer and was working as a lowly second engineer when they first met in March 1983 at AIR Studios, then in Oxford Circus in London's West End, during the mixing of the Too Low For Zero album. Their relationship remained largely dormant until the following Christmas when Elton hired her for the recording of his next album

Marriage

Breaking Hearts at the sister studio to AIR in Montserrat. From there she accompanied him to New Zealand and Australia.

Though painted as a plain Jane, those who knew Renate admired her quiet charisma, sweet nature and sense of humour. She was not a weak person to be easily manipulated. And though there is little doubt she and Elton loved each other, and probably still do, Elton's homosexuality meant they could never be complete as a couple. When Elton came out and confessed to being bisexual he was simply using a euphemism popular at the time in order not to offend his straight audience's sensibilities. He loved women as friends, not sexually. He was homosexual, not bisexual.

Drawn to Renate's strengths and ignoring the inherent incompatibilities, Elton proposed to her over an Indian meal in Sydney and they wed days later at St. Mark's Church in the suburb of Darling Point on St. Valentine's Day, 1984. The bride was aged 30, the groom 36. He was dressed as camply as ever in a straw boater, white tailcoat, purple waistcoat and bow tie. She was in a traditional modest white gown with girlish frilly cuffs and collar and a coronet of flowers. Though smiling and kissing for the cameras, other shots of the wedding show Elton with a puffy face, sweaty and staring.

Later there was a lurid account from Elton's erstwhile gay lover who claimed he went shopping with Renate to choose her dress. Renate's hope that she could clean up Elton's substance abuse proved futile. They tried for the family Elton always said he wanted. His mother expressed her satisfaction at the union – which was an important factor in Elton taking the plunge in the first place.

The rock 'n' roll lifestyle hampered hopes for cosy domesticity with Elton keeping up the pace of touring and recording while Renate remained at home alone when not pursuing her own studio career. Their incompatibilities proved insurmountable and by the end of 1986 their marriage was in trouble and they were in separate bedrooms. When she did not attend his 40th birthday party celebrations in March 1987, Elton was forced to announce their separation. They were to reunite but by November 1988 admitted they were seeking a divorce. Renate was bought Cobblers, a Tudor-style 17th Century cottage in Surrey, and received a settlement believed to be £3 million.

Elton would later say he had a great time being married, but in spite of their mutual love, he had wed for the wrong reasons. Renate could not help him with his own misery and drug problems until he agreed to help himself.

Sad Songs (Say So Much)

Written by: Elton John, Bernie Taupin
Recorded: January 1984, Air Studios, Montserrat
First released: c/w A Simple Man, May 1984

THERE'S NOTHING LIKE A GOOD BLEAT, and Elton's tear ducts are ever ready to oblige. Whether it's Elgar's Nimrod and Enigma Variations or Verdi's Requiem, a good book or film, let alone real life, he is apt to be lachrymose. He loves good death music and writes instrumentals for some of his saddest moments, Song For Guy, Funeral For A Friend, and The Man Who Never Died. Being over-emotional, over-sensitive and prone to a good wallow in self-pity are states Elton can draw on when he wants to put others in that condition - though he assures us he is not morbid.

Singing about a sad song in the abstract, however, is not quite so moving as actually playing one and Elton wisely avoids the obvious trap of writing Sad Songs (Say So Much) as a sad tune because it would not have the desired effect. The melody to Sad Songs is a sprightly affair, a celebration rather than a wake, in a gospel vein. You can imagine Elton declaiming in a church while the backing harmonies testify to his truth.

Bernie's simple lyric is nostalgic, a remembrance of how he has been moved by a sad song on the radio, aware too, that he must have been responsible for doing it to millions himself. Sad Songs is about that little place in one's heart such songs occupy when all else is lost.

Theoretically Elton should not have been too unhappy when recording this over the New Year of 1984. He was falling in love with Renate Blauel, who he insisted should be hired as engineer for the Breaking Hearts album and flown over for the recording sessions in Montserrat.

The album title was originally to be Restless, the name of the opening track. But in the light of his marriage, between recording the album and its release, Elton felt Breaking Hearts was more appropriate. Maybe he had broken the hearts of countless female fans who might have imagined they were the ones who could address his sexual inclinations and take him up the aisle. It was as likely to be aimed at friends, male and female, he felt would

Sad Songs (Say So Much)

consider the marriage a threat to their position in his affections.

The tinkling sound that Elton conjures up on the synthesizer for Sad Songs gives the number the feel of a jingle. And, of course, Elton and Bernie did allow its use as the theme music in a TV commercial for American clothes company Sassons, which employed the slogan 'Sassons say so much'. The pun probably appealed to Elton more than the money.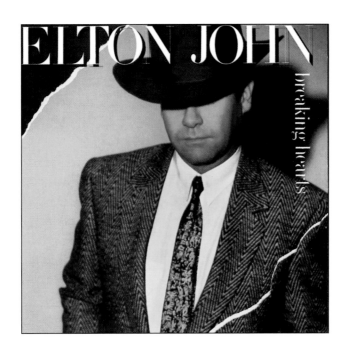

Nikita

Written by: Elton John, Bernie Taupin
Recorded: January 1985, The Mill, Cookham, Berkshire
First released: c/w The Man Who Never Died, October 1985

THE LATE SOVIET PRESIDENT NIKITA KRUSCHEV was a bloke, as are all other Nikitas. This seems to have eluded Bernie Taupin when he was thinking up Nikita. It is unlikely he was trying to put his friend on the spot with an open paean to gay love, especially as Elton was married at the time. Nikita simply tripped off the tongue well, so he became a she, something Ken Russell was happy to play along with in the video he directed, portraying the songs heroine as a blonde Caucasian beauty in Soviet uniform.

It may be an apocryphal story, but Nikita was said to have inspired a cluster of mums in Essex to name their little girls Nikita; something they may come to rue should they ever visit Russia.

The song is set along the Berlin Wall, the story of unrequited love, where

Nikita

Nikita's admirer (capitalist Elton in his Rolls-Royce for the video) can only observe her from behind the barbed wire and hope that one day the wall will come down and she will go west. Substituting the name Renate for Nikita adds an intriguing dimension, adding poignancy to the story of two star-crossed souls.

Out of this bleak landscape Elton devised a melancholy ballad that is seductively simple, gently rising and falling up the scale. He said he could knock out a song like Nikita every day, though he would not want to, as you have to be in the mood. To help him along he brought in some new pop stars: Nik Kershaw on guitar, and George Michael, then still a member of Wham!, singing a beautiful soaring backing soprano. The end product was reminiscent of old style Elton, the carefully honed arrangements the work of producer Dudgeon.

A line from Nikita gave the new album its title, Ice On Fire. It was the first album Elton and Dudgeon had worked on together for over eight years. Elton had initiated the rapprochement presumably hoping he could recreate something of the old feeling. Dudgeon agreed to work on the new album on one condition – that Elton let him vet the songs. Stunned, Elton nevertheless agreed.

Short of making the album an EP however, no amount of quality control could lift the mediocrity of most of the songs. Elton embraced some of the tightly produced bombastic pop grooves that abounded in the mid-Eighties and Nikita was part of a mini-renaissance that was not to last. He succumbed to the problem many artists find when they lose their way, believing studio technique will help mask deficiencies in inspiration.

Nikita reached number three in the British charts, his highest solo chart position since Rocket Man in 1972. It also earned him an Ivor Novello Award, the most coveted of British musicians awards rewarding songwriters, for the year's Best Song Musically and Lyrically and another award for Outstanding Contribution to British Music. The Ice On Fire album repeated the success of Nikita, reaching number three.

The previous album Breaking Hearts had seen the last appearance together of the reformed band from his greatest era, Nigel Olsson, Dee Murray and Davey Johnstone. Gus Dudgeon's return was a relatively brief two years. He was brought in for Ice On Fire's sequel, Leather Jackets, which failed to make the top twenty with its sole single failing to even reach the top forty. EJ

Battling The Press
February 1987.

AS GUTTER PRESS STORIES go it was not so unusual. People were paying for sex, rent boys, bondage and cocaine. The trouble was it was untrue. And *The Sun* picked on someone who unusually had the considerable resources and the will to fight the costly poker game of British libel.

It did not prove that difficult to con the *Sun* into running their so-called exposé. Stephen Hardy was a rent boy later convicted of living off immoral earnings. Under the guise of Graham X, used to supposedly protect his identity, he said he had been paid by Billy Gaff, former manager of Rod Stewart, to have sex with him and Elton John and to procure young rent boys for their pleasure. These sex and drugs orgies were said to have taken place at Gaff's mansion in Finchampstead, Berkshire, not far from Elton's own pile.

Hardy, known as American Barry in his life as a rent boy based at a Soho club, took his tale to the *Sun*. He knew they were sniffing for stories and he was happy to peddle lies to earn a few thousand pounds. The *Sun* were not that interested at first because Hardy was trying to expose Gaff. A more interesting name then came up in his conversations, that of Elton John. Carried away by the tabloid equivalent of feeling you are master of the universe, the *Sun* and its editor Kelvin McKenzie (regarded by many as the most brilliant editor of his generation), printed a story that the paper notably failed, in that unfortunate journalistic phrase, to stand up.

The *Sun*, in common with most British tabloids, has always had a homophobic bent. At the time the first 'Elton In Vice Boys Scandal' headline ran in February 1987, news of Elton's failing marriage had leaked out. In its great tradition of exposing humbug and hypocrisy the *Sun* went for Elton, printing a series of stories on his allegedly sordid double life.

Battling The Press

Unknown to them Elton was an extensive cocaine user at the time, and he later admitted he had paid for sex. Though the facts as they were printed, the dates and the locations and the characters, were fabrications created in a meeting of Hardy's and the newspaper's febrile minds.

The *Sun* also made a major miscalculation with its readership, who regarded Elton as a national treasure, like Vera Lynn and The Queen Mother, and such people were above scandal. Internal memos at News International, owners of the *Sun*, admitted that circulation dropped by as much as 200,000 out of a four million-plus readership on the days Elton stories appeared, rising to normal the next day.

Mick Jagger rang Elton advising him to let it blow over to avoid them raking up more muck. But Elton was not deterred. He fought back on the Michael Parkinson Show telling how the *Sun* had tried to approach his wife's doctor. 'They probably want to examine my sperm. You would have thought they'd have buckets of the stuff.'

The combination of Elton's sharp legal team and the *Sun* going one blunder too far, enabled a swift victory without the need to go to court. The *Sun* alleged Elton had the voice boxes taken out of his Rottweiler dogs. The trouble was he did not have any Rottweilers, and as a renowned dog lover, certainly would not inflict such cruelty on animals. This allegation was far simpler to disprove than the sex and drugs tales which would have involved Elton facing hostile and potentially embarrassing questions in the witness stand. The *Sun* had to concede it would lose any action over the dogs story and that the other allegations were likely to go the same way.

Pressure was being put on the paper by its owner, the much feared Rupert Murdoch. The *Sun* settled and agreed to pay Elton £1 million in damages, plus legal fees estimated at around half that sum again. They published their apology in unprecedented fashion as the major news story of the day, saying the *Sun* and Elton were friends again blaming 'a teenager living in a world of fantasy' for the error. Under the headline 'Sorry Elton' on 12 December, 1988, there is a picture of a fragile looking star putting on a brave, and it appears forced, smile.

Five years later he was to win another libel battle, this time with the *Sunday Mirror*, who falsely alleged that he was showing signs of bulimia, the illness he had by then overcome. It cost the paper £350,000.

Elton has said that suing the media has become a hobby. His reasoning is straight-forward enough. 'They can say I'm a fat old sod. They can say I'm an untalented bastard. They can call me a poof. But they mustn't lie about me because then I'm going to fight. And I'm determined to be a winner.'

I Don't Wanna Go On With You Like That

Written by: Elton John, Bernie Taupin
Recorded: January 1988, Air Studios, London
First released: c/w Rope Around A Fool, May 1988

THE JAUNTINESS OF I Don't Wanna Go On With You Like That and the defiantly upbeat tone of the album Reg Strikes Back are attempts to gloss over the feelings of depression and self-loathing that characterised Elton's state of mind that annus horribilis, 1987. Q magazine called it, 'what may well have been the worst year a pop star has ever been through and lived'.

I Don't Wanna... has all the hallmarks of a man with a brave face putting it on. You can sense his dimpled chin jutting out. The chords slam over a monotonous dance beat that is almost military in its regularity. He could be at that old jangle joanna again, trying to get everyone to pack up their bags of woe and have a right old knees up.

Elton's fear of going into the studio at the end of 1987/beginning 1988 was that his depression would translate on to tape and he would end up writing a lot of 'those bloody slow songs'. In the end it proved the opposite and he said it was a happy album to make. At the time he even thought it reminiscent of his Goodbye Yellow Brick Road era. It had energy, but lacked memorable tunes, veering through a hotch potch of styles from Flamenco to Motown to Caribbean. He was later to announce his dissatisfaction with the results. I Don't Wanna... only got to number thirty in Britain. In America it got to number two, kept off the top spot by Elton's mate and new protégé, George Michael.

The lyrics to I Don't Wanna... relate a bland tale of serial betrayal except for one

I Don't Wanna Go On With You Like That

verse that alludes to things getting out of hand and having a momentum of their own. If Bernie was choosing to be obtuse regarding his friend's plight he did it convincingly throughout Reg Strikes Back. In Bernie's own special way the song Goodbye Marlon Brando touches on media saturation and the need to escape, while Town Of Plenty describes a feeling of alienation from a place that once felt like home. It was Elton himself who chose to make the most direct reference to his experiences through his choice of the album title itself, Reg Strikes Back. He was striking back at the British press. He was reclaiming his once despised old name in an attempt to make himself whole. The album artwork was a studio shot of his collected belongings before they were auctioned by Sotheby's two months after the record's release. He was trying to reduce the clutter in his life, both external and internal and start afresh.

Elton's crisis year had begun with an operation while in Australia to remove nodules from his throat. The newspapers had screamed 'cancer', convinced his voice box was to be removed. In the event the lesions taken from his vocal chords proved benign.

The following month the Sun newspaper splashed the first headlines in its notorious campaign accusing Elton of paying rent boys for sex followed by an allegation that he kept Rottweiler dogs who had their voice boxes removed. He felt under a state of siege stuck in his house in Old Windsor after the Sun allegations and could not stop crying. At the same time his marriage to Renate was expiring. His sense of unease was exacerbated by eating disorders and continued use of alcohol and cocaine.

It took him six months to get his voice back, which even before the operation was worn out to the extent that he had lost his falsetto. And anyway he was in no mood to work.

In November 1987 he saw on television the courage and forgiveness of Gordon Wilson who had been with his daughter as she died besides him in a bombing in Enniskillen, Northern Ireland. For Elton it put his own plight into perspective. His strong survival instincts made him realise the best way to claw his way back into the world was doing what he knew best, music. Reg Strikes Back was the result.

Mine All Mine
Sotheby's Sale, September 1988.

DEFYING ALL BRITISH NOTIONS OF DECORUM AND TASTE, Elton revels in his ability
to use consumerism as his remaining great addiction. He could no more imagine
no possessions than he could grow hair on his crown.

For Elton his wealth is to be enjoyed and shared. He has a healthy attitude that
money lying around serves no-one, and though his acquisitions may not always be
in the best possible taste they are invariably exuberant and life-affirming.

His materialism stems from childhood needs. Not so much any deprivation
during his modest beginnings in Pinner, more his solitariness. Being a lone child
with a protective mother and an often absent and hostile father, objects became
his friends. He believed they had feelings, and still does, remembering when they
make him happy. Little Reg liked to catalogue his discs, putting his name on them
and never lending them out in case they got scratched or lost. It was his way of
controlling his environment. He might not be able to rely on the affections of
people, but objects were always loyal.

In adulthood he objectified his relationships and would talk of boyfriends being
'Eltonized', ultimately meaning they would be sent on their way with a Cartier
watch and Versace shirt. He spread his wealth round to friends and staff, buying
expensive gifts and holding parties that Press speculation put at costs of tens, if
not hundreds, of thousands of pounds.

He has been rich since his early twenties, building up clutter in his various
homes, first a luxury flat at the Water Gardens off the Edgware Road in London,
then at Hercules, his bungalow in Virginia Water, and then at Woodside, his Queen
Anne-style mansion in Old Windsor. His other homes are a town house in Holland

Mine All Mine

Park, West London, a series of adjoining apartments in Atlanta, Georgia and most recently the Castel Mont-Alban villa in the Côte d'Azur. To these belongings can be added fleets of limousines, his peripatetic boutique-sized wardrobe, books and works of art.

In 1988, wanting to clear out the expensive detritus that had gathered around him, he held a sale at Sotheby's auction house in London which brought in over £4.8 million. The four catalogues of possessions revealed a hit and miss taste, some elegant, some exciting, and some rubbish. There were Magrittes and L.S. Lowrys, an erotic table by Allen Jones, Lalique and Tiffany lamps, old gold discs and his Eiffel Tower boater, his nearly five foot high Doc Marten boots from the movie *Tommy*, a replica of Tutankhamun's throne, and jewellery that would have shamed Elizabeth Taylor.

He had intended to leave Woodside but instead in the early Nineties had its interior ripped apart. Gone is the clutter and in its place, designer themed rooms from antique to neo-deco with his replacement collection of art and furniture showing a more disciplined and educated taste. He had an Italian garden designed by Sir Roy Strong, the former director of the Victoria and Albert Museum, and employs two full-time arrangers who keep the house ablaze and perfumed with flowers.

Watford Football Club was another possession, an indulgence to satisfy his ego but also a chance to pay back some of his good fortune. He was to apply the same drive and energy he put into being a pop star into the team he had supported since childhood. From the start of his chairmanship in 1976 he was to finance in the millions the club's rise from the Fourth to the First Division and on to the Wembley F.A. Cup Final in 1984, selling up in 1990 before taking up the chairman-ship again in 1997, this time more wisely spreading the risk as part of a consortium.

His spending has never abated. His money undoubtedly gives him automatic power, enabling hime to control the retinue who make his life run smoothly. As was obvious in David Furnish's documentary *Tantrums And Tiaras*, there are still plenty of fawning gophers willing to cow-tow to his whims. But he is sensitive to accusations that he buys friends and says he sees his long-term staff as family. In the drug days everyone was his friend because he controlled the stash. These days he appears more discerning, though in his case at least, he disproves that hack-neyed maxim that money can't buy you happiness. EJ

An Honorary Royal
Dancing with The Windsors, February 1989.

ONCE THE ROYALS WOULD LOOK DOWN their sizeable noses at the rock 'n' roll rabble who excited the nation's youth. The impression from Buckingham Palace was that one was best advised to let them eat coke, as it were.

Elton John always was an exception, however. He first played for royalty in 1972 at a benefit concert attended by Princess Margaret and later in the year for The Queen, at a Royal Variety Command Performance on a bill that included Liberace. Elton's music and image fitted all the right criteria; he was melodious, not too loud, non-political, and a showman.

Before long he was invited into the Royal palaces, giving intimate performances for the Queen Mother and Princess Margaret. He was literally caught with his trousers down at Windsor Castle by Margaret who walked in on him as he was changing out of a costume. He befriended Margaret, going to the cinema with her and inviting her to bring the kids down the road to his pad within sight of their rather larger one at Windsor Castle. He would later become one of the best customers for Viscount Linley, Margaret's son, when he became a master furniture.

Wherever royalty goes, inevitably controversy follows, and Elton found it did not do to break protocol by telling the Press what had been divulged to one. When Princess Alexandra asked him, after a concert at the Rainbow Theatre in London in 1977, if he had taken cocaine, he told the Press about it.

In 1981 he performed at Windsor Castle for Prince Andrew's 21st birthday party. It was here he first met Lady Diana Spencer. Later that year he was a guest at her marriage to Prince Charles whose Prince's Trust he has supported with several performances. The best example of how popular and trusted he was came at a royal party in 1989. He arrived at the ballroom in Windsor Castle to find no-one

An Honorary Royal

was there except the dance band and Princess Diana. They danced the Charleston alone for 20 minutes. Then Princess Anne asked him if he would like to dance. 'What am I going to say? "No-clear off?" We went into this disco where the music was so quiet, you could hardly hear it. As we're bopping up and down, the Queen comes up with an equerry and says, "Do you mind if we join you?" Just at that moment, the music goes into Bill Haley. So I'm dancing to Rock Around The Clock with the Queen of England.'

When long-time fan Sarah Ferguson married Prince Andrew, Elton's gift included a tape of a specially-composed piano instrumental, because she had told him her favourite song was the instrumental Song For Guy. Andrew and Sarah and Elton and Renate regularly dined together and attended each others bashes.

It was with Diana though, that he was to share the greatest bond. After his recovery and his increased commitment to charity they became more involved in each other's projects until they fell out in the months before her death.

Diana had agreed to write the forward to a book called *Rock And Royalty* devised by Gianni Versace with profits going to Elton's AIDS foundation. She pulled out under pressure from the Palace, offended that pictures of royalty sat alongside photos of semi-nude models in bondage gear. Versace cancelled the launch and made a donation instead.

Elton was furious because Diana had not informed him before he read of it in the Press. He sent her a sniffy letter and she sent one back notoriously starting, "Dear Mr John..." He tried to smooth it over by phoning her but she refused to take his calls. Diana relented in July 1997 when she phoned him after hearing of Versace's death. The picture of her arm around a sobbing Elton at the funeral service in Milan became even more poignant when she was to die a month later.

Elton had been mooted for an honour for years and in 1996 was made a Commander of the British Empire for his services to music and charity. After his Candle In The Wind 1997 performance which was expected to make £100 million, Prime Minister Tony Blair thought it would be a popular move to finally give Elton a knighthood.

On 24 February, 1998 the head of the Queen's Household, Lord Camoys, the Lord Chamberlain, announced "Sir John Elton" as Elton walked up to kneel before the Queen in Buckingham Palace and receive his dubbing. Clearly some things had not changed in the Palace. Lord Camoys was unfamiliar with the celebrity of the new Knight Bachelor, changing his name round because he thought it was written down incorrectly.

Healing Hands

Written by: Elton John, Bernie Taupin
Recorded: November and December 1988, Puk Studios, Denmark
First released: c/w Dancing in the End Zone, August 1989

ELTON'S SQUAT BUT FINELY CHISELLED HANDS are everywhere in Herb Ritts'
pictures used on the Sleeping With The Past album. They are wrapped around
his head in shadow on the sepia front cover. In the CD booklet they are pictured palms down as if ready to strike the piano, and in another shot, widened,
making them appear lifeless on a slab. They symbolised Elton grappling
towards a solution to the personal turmoil that had climaxed in the last few
years and his new determination to resolve the crises.

 The mood of Healing Hands is sombre, but also uplifting. A soulful ballad in
keeping with the R&B theme of the album, it is Elton stepping out from behind
the organ he played in Bluesology and taking the microphone from the hand of
Major Lance or Lee Dorsey who fronted shows he backed in the Sixties. One of
the song's influences was The Four Tops' hit Reach Out, I'll Be There, and in fact
includes the words 'reach out' in the lyrics. There is a calm reflection in Elton's
voice. Building from the gentle start he crescendos and staccatos, opening up
his vocal chords for the chorus helped by his backing singers. He uses an organ
effect on the synthesizer with a run of harpsichord-like notes. It is a melange of
his earliest influences and styles.

Healing Hands

The healing hands of the song belong to a woman who can cure the pain. Of course this was no longer applicable in a literal sense to Elton, once more reconciled to his homosexuality in the wake of his failed marriage. More than anything it is a song of resolve and positivity, of never giving in to the darkness. In that sense it is similar to the album's title track, the gospel styled Sleeping With The Past, urging a woman who is prone to go for the wrong type of man to shake off the bad habits off a lifetime, to put the past to sleep.

The album was an effort by Elton and Bernie to break their own past patterns of songwriting. Elton was concerned that they had been going through the motions, putting out too much mediocre material. Bernie based himself in England more than was usual and together they decided on the 'white-black' theme, white boys doing the black music they grew up listening to, the nearest they had gotten to a concept since Goodbye Yellow Brick Road. Bernie went back to listen to Jackie Wilson, Sam and Dave, Otis Redding and the rest. Discussing their work they also talked about their lives and felt closer than they had for some time. Elton was not yet sober and Bernie was going through the failure of his second marriage.

Rather than the lyrics landing on Elton's piano stand, they thrashed out what they wanted to achieve in each song before Bernie wrote the lyrics to fit in with Elton's idea for a melody. For Bernie, having taught himself guitar and how to compose his own tunes, it was a breakthrough in the way he felt Elton regarded his contribution on a musical level, after more than twenty years of writing together.

The songs finally fell into place during the recording sessions in Denmark and the influences poured out – The Drifters on Club At The End Of The Street, Marvin Gaye on Stone's Throw From Hurtin, Ray Charles on Amazes Me. Lee Dorsey's Working In The Coalmine gave Bernie the idea for the lyric to Durban Deep, about diamond mining in South Africa, even though it was given a reggae beat.

Both were pleased with the outcome. For Bernie, no album they had ever made contained so many strong songs. He was proud of its integrity and was sure it was commercial. The first single, Healing Hands, was not to reward Bernie's faith, floundering at number forty-five in the chart. 🎹

Sacrifice

Written by: Elton John, Bernie Taupin
Recorded: November and December 1988, Puk Studios, Denmark
First Released: Healing Hands Album, September 1989

AS LATE AS NOVEMBER 1989 Elton was quoted as saying he did not expect he would ever get a number one in Britain, which he regarded as just about his least successful market in the world. When he recorded the Sleeping With The Past album in the studio the consensus, minus Elton, was that Sacrifice was surely a hit. For a change Elton looked like being proved right. The single failed to even reach the top fifty in Britain, though it made the top twenty in America.

Although regarded affectionately as a national institution (even more so after his public tribulations), Elton's days as a force in pop appeared to be over. In the past he managed hits with sub-standard songs or albums, now he was having a miss with a quality composition.

Bernie regarded Sacrifice as a far superior work to Your Song, which people often refer to as his standard. For him, Your Song was a naive song written by an inexperienced teen. Sacrifice was the song of a 40-year-old man who had

Sacrifice

been through failed marriages and disastrous sexual conquests. At its core, its 'cold heart', the song is brutal. It is called Sacrifice but it is a lament about being insensitive to what you sacrifice when others suffer as a result of your pursuit of self-gratification. It is knowing and clearly autobiographical.

Elton sings it self-pityingly, his voice muted and the arrangement kept simple to draw out the emotion. The stately, sustained organ sound emphasises the pathos as the tale unfolds, while it is propelled by a sweet soul rhythm.

Elton thought of Percy Sledge when he composed the melody for the song. The lyrics were initially influenced by Aretha Franklin singing Do Right Woman, Do Right Man, even though the final lyrics and tune ended up a long way from this source.

Sacrifice would have been yet another footnote in Elton's long list of releases had it not been for Steve Wright, a DJ at Radio One, who got hooked on the song while driving on holiday in Florida. On his return he played Sacrifice repeatedly on his show, prompting the record company to re-release it as a double A-side with another flop, Healing Hands. Its ascent was fast and it reached number one in June 1990, where it stayed for four weeks.

It was Elton's first British solo number one single in nineteen years of chart success. In its wake the album Sleeping With The Past also reached number one. It felt like the culmination of his old life, enabling a new one to start.

Earlier that year he had been deeply moved by the courage and death at 18 of Ryan White, a haemophiliac who had contracted the AIDS virus through a blood transfusion and had been ostracised at school and forced to move towns. Elton stayed with Ryan at his death and organised the funeral. Witnessing his family's humility and generosity was crucial in helping Elton re-evaluate his own life. He had also reached a crisis with his boyfriend Hugh Williams whose decision to check himself into a detoxification clinic had at first infuriated Elton. He soon realised, however, that he had no choice but to do the same.

When Sacrifice reached number one Elton felt his good fortune should be shared and pledged all profits from Sacrifice, and the profits of all future Elton John singles, would go to HIV/AIDS charities. At the end of July as Sacrifice slipped from its glorious peak on the British charts, Elton booked himself into the Parkside Lutheran Hospital, Chicago, to finally deal with his alcoholism, cocaine addiction, compulsive eating and bulimia.

Drugs
Recovery begins, July 1990.

IT WAS INEVITABLE that during the process of recovery Elton would look back to his childhood for the source of his multiple addictions. He was sure, yet again, that his father had a hand in it. As a child he locked himself in his room when his parents rowed. He would do everything he could to avoid confrontations with people, which led him to become shy and withdrawn. He concluded that this had been the start of the process which led to his addictions.

In adult life it was drink that first allowed him to be as uninhibited in social situations as he had learnt to become on stage. In his first years of success he shunned drugs, but their prevalence, combined with his feeling of being excluded, eventually led him to try them.

Heroin was for real drug addicts. Marijuana was all right. But it was cocaine that he fell in love with. As late as 1998 he spoke of being able to cope with people drinking around him, but had to leave the room if someone chopped out a line of Charlie, because part of him would like it too much.

Cocaine, as Sting told him, was God's way of telling you that you have too much money. Like Sigmund Freud before him, Elton was fooled into thinking the eloquence and insight cocaine gave him was profound, when in reality it was bullshit. For a man already possessed with demonic amounts of energy, Bolivian marching powder simply made him manic.

The strains of fame and touring plus the onset of serious substance abuse first became publicly visible in April 1974, when Elton canceled a European tour. Asked a few years later what his memory was of that period, he said he had none. Which was also applicable to many longer periods. The scale of his drug use varied, sometimes he was able to give up

Drugs

for six months, but then would slide into it again. By the late Seventies it had reached critical levels that would continue for another decade. He was not a pleasant person to be around. A self-confessed 'nasty, vicious drunk', his booze of choice was champagne, vodka martinis and mostly Johnnie Walker Black Label whisky.

He could go on three-day cocaine benders. Where a normal user would share a gram, Elton would do whole ounce bags. He would hide away in his bedroom, bingeing on cocaine and whisky, watching pornographic movies. He described it as 'being the most alone you can be'.

When not confined to the privacy of his home, he became impossible to please, complaining about the colour of his private jet, the furniture or bed covers in his hotel suites, and on one occasion the very wind outside – he phoned hotel reception to demand that they do something about it.

It was not all grim, however. Cocaine was atypically a great aphrodisiac allowing him to play out his sexual fantasies. But, of course, sex then became another addiction.

While 'on' cocaine he would not eat for days. Then, when he was coming down, he would gorge himself on jars of cockles, bacon sandwiches, pints of ice-cream and curries. He would make himself sick, and then start again. He took Dialantin, a muscle relaxant prescribed for seizures, snorting coke again within minutes of his heart calming down.

Though there was an inevitable set of druggie hangers-on, his dearest friends and family were constantly urging him to seek treatment. Unable to cope, his mother moved to Spain in the mid-Eighties. He knew he had a problem but he wanted to solve it for himself, seeing anything else as a sign of weakness. It was only when he realized that he needed help that he was able to start on his recovery.

Simply having to share a room at the Parkside Lutheran Hospital in Chicago was tough enough – and there were times when he would sit on the pavement outside determined to leave – but he knew he had nowhere left to go. His treatment included writing a farewell letter to cocaine. After six weeks he returned to England and joined the 12-Step Alcoholics Anonymous programme which he stayed on for three years. He started using the language of recovery with its talk of a 'Higher Power'. He took to starting his days by meditating, attending endless meetings and holding early morning sessions with other recovering addicts in his own home. Just seeing the daylight and the beauty of sunsets were revelations for him.

As he was once addicted to drugs and alcohol, so Elton is now addicted to honesty. The life he kept so hidden from view he has exposed himself in various courageous interviews and the *Tantrums And Tiaras* documentary. It satisfies our curiosity and arouses empathy. The act of communicating, in the jargon 'sharing', helps him affirm his new life.

The One

Written by: Elton John, Bernie Taupin

Recorded: Between November 1991 and March 1992, Studio Guillaume Tell, Paris

First Released: c/w Suit of Wolves, May 1992

SOBRIETY GAVE ELTON JOHN HIS LIFE BACK, but it did not even out his notorious moods. The One was his first studio album to be completed while he was unclouded by drugs and drink since the early Seventies. He found the prospect fearsome and lasted just twenty minutes in the studio on his first day. The album would eventually be completed after five months of on-and-off recording. A very different schedule to the previous routines of no more than two weeks.

This time, he and Bernie reverted to the practice they had abandoned on Sleeping With The Past, with Bernie delivering lyrics without prior discussion. The One was a special and rare song for Bernie Taupin. His habit was to write songs that featured composites of people and experiences he had come across. He was newly in love, however, with Stephanie Haymes, a restaurateur from Los Angeles, who was later to become his third wife, and The One is about their relationship. For him she was the love of his life, the one we all search for.

The lyrics are shamelessly romantic, with their Hollywood gloss of running along the beach and of true love as an epiphany. There's a sly look back to his previous fallen lifestyle before the world is put to rights with the rousing chorus and images of wild horses, clouds falling away and colliding stars.

Elton was happy to go along with the kitsch imagery. There is the sound of seagulls and the ocean rushing in as the song opens and builds to the anthemic climax. He sings like an overwrought tenor tackling an auspicious aria. Like the rest of the album, under the capable - if stodgy - stewardship of Chris Thomas, it is slickly executed. The One stands out because most of the other tunes are bland and no amount of window dressing can rescue them. The package itself was dressed by Elton's new great friend, the Italian maestro of haute-couture, Gianni Versace. He came up with the album 'cover concept' of purple red and gold rococo flourishes. Versace also designed the

stage set and outfits for Elton and his band for the 1992 tour.

The face staring out of the album cover was familiar, though the thatch was not. This was Elton showing off his new £14,000 hair weave. With its schoolboy fringe emphasised by his round spectacles he looked younger, pensive and refreshingly clear-eyed.

It was not a straightforward equation where simply by purging his system of impurities Elton could rekindle his creative powers. But the album was good enough for a public that had recently warmed again to his music. His live duet with George Michael of Don't Let The Sun Go Down On Me had gone to number one in Britain and America, and Two Rooms, an album of other artists covering his songs had also got to number one. The One continued this happy comeback, reaching number ten in Britain and number eight in America, where it became his most successful album since Blue Moves in 1976.

The Last Song

Written by: Elton John, Bernie Taupin
Recorded: Between November 1991 and March 1992, Studio Guillaume Tell, Paris
First Released: The One album, June 1992

FATE COULD EASILY HAVE DEALT ELTON JOHN the hand it cruelly dished to Rock Hudson, Liberace, Freddie Mercury, several of his close friends and hundreds of thousands more. Unprotected gay sex combined with a compromised immune system thanks to copious amounts of cocaine and bulimia rendered Elton a prime candidate to catch the HIV/AIDS virus. That he avoided infection was a blessing he was never to forget and would lead to him becoming one of the world's foremost campaigners for the care of sufferers.

Conscious of Elton's strong feelings, Bernie wrote a song that, though not to order, he was sure his mouthpiece would be happy to enunciate. He composed it soon after the death of Freddie Mercury, the singer from Queen who was a great friend and sometime rival of Elton, in November 1991. The Last Song, in a lyrical sense only, could be traced back to Marty Robbins' El Paso. It is a novella in song of an AIDS victim able to die in peace after his reconciliation with a father who he thought was not able to accept him and his disease. It is mawkish and morbid, unavoidably so, but it has a touching simplicity and universality. It is not Bernie's finest lyric, possibly because he was guided more by his head than his heart. He wanted to make a song that was acceptable to middle-America. If he had written a purely gay song featuring two lovers it would have no chance of the exposure it enjoyed as a father-son crisis. He said his intention was not a cry for help so much as a plea for greater awareness.

Elton was crying as he wrote the music in the studio. He broke down when he recorded the demo, crying and crying. He was crying for Freddie, for his friends, and for his father, who had also recently died (in December 1991), and with whom Elton was never fully reconciled, a situation he partly blamed himself for.

Starting with the word 'yesterday' the song sounds momentarily like it might be the Paul McCartney classic. It progresses as a dirge in the style of Andrew

The Last Song

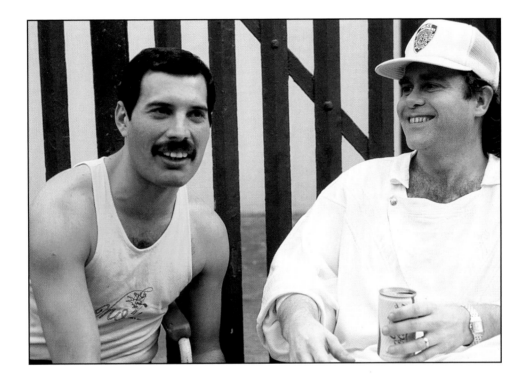

Lloyd-Webber. Elton's deep voice summoning the spirits of those he has lost, rising, hymn-like to a synthesizer sound of pan-pipes. He rescues the song through the sheer intensity of his emotions.

In 1976 Elton John had been brave enough to confess to being gay. In 1992 when The Last Song was released, he was one of the few major artists willing to tackle the topic of AIDS in song, singing as the voice of a gay man, and risk yet again the wrath of that chunk of his audience that did not welcome such themes into their living rooms. It was a modest hit, reaching number twenty-three in America and twenty-one in Britain. For Elton this was a new coming out. He had never been taken with political causes, but AIDS aroused his passions like no cause before and he was unwilling to dilute the message.

The Elton John AIDS Foundation
December 1992

NEVER ONE TO ESPOUSE CAUSES BEFORE, Elton found, in the AIDS pandemic, an issue that affected him personally; through the loss of friends and because it was a gay issue, the gay community being the first group to suffer its curse. It was also a human rights issue because of prejudice and the legal consequences for sufferers. Plus, Elton was simply grateful that he had managed to avoid a virus despite his own actions having put him in a high risk category.

The Elton John AIDS Foundation

He was first motivated to take a public stand on AIDS when he heard of the case of Ryan White, a teenage haemophiliac infected with the virus from tainted blood products. White had attracted a lot of celebrity support when he was ostracized at school and church in his Indiana home town and forced to move house. Elton made contact in late 1986 when he heard that he was the celebrity Ryan most wanted to meet. He put on special treats for Ryan and in April 1990 kept a week-long vigil at his bedside as he lay dying. Elton had become close to Ryan's family, was moved by Ryan and his mother's humility and refusal to be bitter. He organized the funeral and sang Skyline Pigeon at the service.

A year after Ryan's death Elton met another American, Elizabeth Glaser, the founder of the Pediatric AIDS Foundation. Glaser had lost one child to AIDS while she and a surviving child were HIV Positive. Inspired by her charity and with his own demons behind him, in late 1992 Elton formed The Elton John AIDS Foundation in Los Angeles and London.

Drawing on his experience of running Watford F.C. he became chairman of the Foundation setting up executive and advisory boards. As with everything in his life, he wanted to be in control. And as with Watford, he wanted a project that would relieve him of his own self-absorption.

Having performed at charity concerts since the early days, he was aware how much money can disappear with hospitality and hotel bills etc. and so runs the foundation on a frugal basis. Its brief is to maintain the quality of life for sufferers and educate people at risk.

The money from his single releases is channeled into the Foundation, as are frequent sales of his clothes. There are also a range of endorsed products – all very Elton – that include a Lalique cherub, limited edition Oliver Peoples spectacles, an Elton Candle, collectible pre-paid phone cards and gothic jewelry, a proportion of all profits from which are donated to the Foundation. There is also an Elton John AIDS Foundation Visa card issued by MBNA America Bank, who give a donation for every purchase made with it. All of which has enabled the Foundation to become one of the world's largest charities in the field.

Can You Feel The Love Tonight
Written by: Elton John, Tim Rice
Recorded: During 1993 and 1994, Townhouse Studio, London, and Olympic Studio, London
First Released: The Lion King album, June 1994

AS ELTON WAS ACCLIMATISING TO STUDIO LIFE in the summer of 1991 from the strained perspective of a recovering addict, he received a call from Walt Disney Pictures. Was he interested in collaborating with Tim Rice on songs for a new cartoon animation to be called *The Lion King*? In his heightened state of capriciousness it was hard to predict what Elton's attitude might be.

A meeting was set up in London between Elton, Rice and Tom Schumacher, a Walt Disney executive vice-president. Expecting the hard sell, Schumacher instead found an enthusiastic Elton keen to expand his creative scope.

Tim Rice was a golden boy for Disney, after the success of his work on the *Aladdin* cartoon. Asked who would be his chosen collaborator for *The Lion King*, Rice instinctively thought of Elton despite having never discussed the project with him.

Their previous effort had not shown much flare. Tim Rice had come up with contorted lyrics and Elton an over-excited tune for the song Legal Boys which appeared on the underwhelming Jump Up album of 1982. Elton's only film experience was in 1971 with the release of the soundtrack, a project that perversely brought out the mediocre in him just as his creativity was starting to flower.

The *Lion King* project was to prove of great benefit for Elton in his recovery. The disciplines of team work were a revelation for a man shielded for so long in an autocratic fiefdom. Elton was to describe the resulting two-year project as one of the most enjoyable experiences of his life. He liked being brought storyboards and asked to write or adapt his melodies as the action evolved. It was the process of consultation that appealed to him.

Fortunately for himself and Disney, they took note of what he had to say. When the film was nearly finished the track Can You Feel The Love Tonight was removed from the movie along with the love scene between the cubs

Can You Feel The Love Tonight

Simba and Nala. Elton told them, 'you could not have a Disney movie without a love scene, or love song'. His advice was heeded.

Elton wrote The Circle Of Life, the movie's main theme, in about 90 minutes. It's lyrical theme of wholeness and resolution were echoed in Elton's own existence. Can You Feel The Love Tonight is a conventional lyric with all of the light and none of the shadow of a Bernie Taupin creation. As was the convention with Bernie, Rice wrote his lyrics separately and presented them to Elton. Unlike Legal Boys where Rice was attempting to be edgy, Can You Feel reverts to his natural smooth eloquence. Elton responded with a creamy ballad that milks the romance and establishes the requisite heart-tugging resolution. Elton wrote an accessible hummable tune conscious that the core audience were children, an aspect of the process he enjoyed having always felt empathy with them.

The backstage tension of the 1995 Academy Awards ceremony in Hollywood was caught on video by Elton's lover David Furnish in his voyeuristic and riveting documentary *Tantrums And Tiaras*. Elton has a quick snooze in his Winnebago trailer while awaiting the results. After performing Can You Feel The Love Tonight the moment comes, announced by Sylvester Stallone, awarding Elton John and Tim Rice the Oscar for Best Song. Elton described it as one of the proudest moments of his life and in his acceptance speech dedicated his Oscar to his grandmother Ivy Sewell, who had died the week before. 'She was the one who sat me down at the piano when I was three and made me play,' he said.

In November 1997 *The Lion King* was premiered to rapturous acclaim as a Broadway stage musical, adapted by Elton John and Tim Rice. Their movie partnership continues with a second cartoon animation, , in conjunction with Hans Zimmer, who scored . This was commissioned by Jeffrey Katzenberg, who oversaw *The Lion King* at Disney and was now co-owner of the DreamWorks studio with Steven Spielberg and Elton's former American record company boss, David Geffen. Elton is exploring further movie and stage projects. With Rice he has adapted the opera *Aida* as a stage musical, while he and Bernie plan to adapt Captain Fantastic And The Brown Dirt Cowboy into a West End musical. [EJ]

Made In England

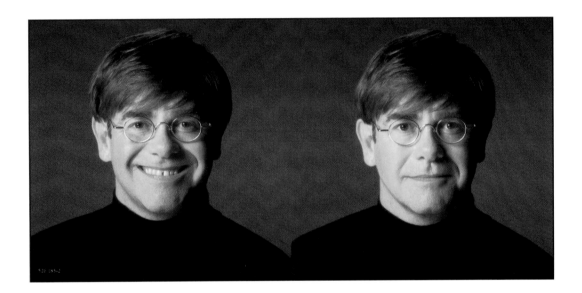

Made In England

Recorded: Between February and May 1994, AIR Lyndhurst Hall Studios
First released: Made In England album, March 1995

IT'S NOT JUST SAINSBURY'S COCKLES, Marks and Spencer's muffins, HP Sauce and Coleman's English mustard. It's not just Kenneth Williams and Beryl Reid, Alan Bennett and *The Goon Show*. It's not just Watford Football Club and Pinner and gardening. It is not just royalty and honours and Hush Puppies and stiff upper lips and limp wrists. But it is the ineffable confluence of all these things that defines Elton John's Englishness.

He has always been a patriot, with a small p, defending his country and moaning about it but never deserting it. It is his Englishness that has allowed him to reinterpret R&B and rock 'n' roll from a perspective that makes it palatable to a wider and whiter world.

Up to the last minute the Made In England album was going to be called Believe, the opening track, until Elton decided it made the album sound too mystic. The album was made in England, and so was Elton and that was the name of a track, so the new title seemed most appropriate.

On the song Made In England Bernie, long resident in California, put himself into Elton's frame of mind, succinctly drawing, in words, the essential Elton: the 'Cadillac' and 'Cortina'; 'Little Richard' and 'Elvis; the boy from Tupelo'. There's mention of the dad who left and love for his mum. And there's a swipe at how the English deal with gays by turning them into figures of camp fun.

The 'Wow oh oh oh' singalong chorus of Made In England would not sound out of place on a football terrace. The tune itself is a raucous pub rock 'n' roller full of Davey Johnstone's jingling guitar and Elton's coarse vocal, culminating in a rousing 'Eng[er]land'.

Here was a different Elton. Mercurial as of old, no doubt, but healing, too. The songs have cryptic titles that make the album appear starker than it is. Believe was written by Taupin about the decay of his father's cancer, but it is underscored with a belief in the triumph of love. It is put over with great warmth helped by the arrangements of Paul Buckmaster who was brought back for four numbers. The song House is an affectionate celebration of the sanctity of one's home. It was played on the documenatry of *Tantrums And Tiaras* as Elton was rejoicing on his return to his Berkshire home. There are jarring moments on the album, notably a patronising ode to the strength of the people in Belfast. Bernie can be blamed for that one. Overall though, a sense of care and concentration went into all aspects of this album.

Elton co-produced with Greg Penny, whose work he had admired on k.d.lang's sensuous Ingenue album and who worked with her on Elton's Duets album. Spending more time and taking more care in the studio than he had done since 1976, Elton whittled down 20 songs to 11 and never let one go until he was pleased with every aspect of it. The simplicity of the album cover, with a happy and 'at ease' Elton, was proof that he had found his way back. EJ

ELTON JOHN

THE BIG PICTURE

The Big Picture

Recorded: Between March and July 1997 at The Town House Studios
First released: The Big Picture album, September 1997

THE YEAR OF 1997 WAS ALWAYS going to be a momentous one, marking as it did, both 30 years of Elton and Bernie writing songs together and Elton's 50th birthday. Yet ultimately it was profound personal tragedy and not achievement or stamina, which defined it.

As the finishing touches were being made to The Big Picture, Elton's first album in over two years, he heard the news that Gianni Versace, the friend with whom he spoke every day, had been assassinated on the steps of his Miami home. Versace had become perhaps Elton's closest muse, along with the new love of his life, advertising account director turned film maker, David Furnish.

As if a harbinger of these-heart-wrenching events, The Big Picture was full mostly of contemplative songs about the human condition and relationships. The album is ballad-heavy, mixing melancholia with hope and happiness springing eternal. It is devoid of Bernie's customary adventurers and shady characters and is instead full of imagery of the natural world: twisting and turning rivers and oceans, clouds and stars, animals and weather.

The title song is an affectionate look at a long-standing relationship, where hopes are expressed that the warm friendship will continue. It is a meditation from a mature Brown Dirt Cowboy on his bond with Captain Fantastic summed up in the final lines of the chorus, '...I've been up all night looking at the big picture/I've got some good lines for my big star.' It is a suitably cinematic rock ballad with strings for extra expansiveness and Elton savouring each word as he rolls it out. It is grand in its ambitions, while still conveying deep fondness.

As with Made In England, a sense of care and attention to detail permeates the album. There are atmospheres pregnant with portentousness. The End Will Come, for example, in the light of later events, came to have deeper resonance. The intention, however, was to write songs along the lines of classic standards sung by Frank Sinatra or Tony Bennett. Something About The Way You Look Tonight, which was to become the double A-side with Candle In The Wind 1997, comes closest to achieving this.

Having now got into the habit of discussing what they were setting out to achieve, Elton stipulated one condition. He did not want to be singing boy-girl songs, which he thought no longer sounded convincing to an audience that knew he was 'out'. Instead, there is ambiguity as to whether the songs are boy-to-boy or boy-to-girl.

Instead of stream-of-consciousness from an aspiring poet laureate, Elton now gets carefully structured songs that Bernie has written with a view to the melody. Having sung it in his own head, Bernie will give Elton his idea for the melody, which Elton will either heed or discard. Instead of scoring out lines or whole verses regardless of Bernie's feelings. Elton will now consult him on changes and not do anything Bernie does not like.

Elton John and Bernie Taupin have both defied the urge to self-destruct that so often befalls intense creative partnerships. And though they are unlikely to repeat the god-like classics of the Seventies, they are still capable of work that is relevant, modern and moving. EJ

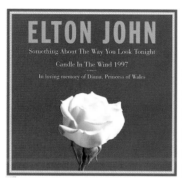

Candle In The Wind 1997

Recorded: 6 September, 1997, The Town House Studios

First Released: c/w double a-side Something About The Way You Look Tonight and You Can Make History (Young Again), 13 September, 1997

BUCKINGHAM PALACE AND THE CHURCH OF ENGLAND were not sure that they wanted Elton John to perform at the funeral service in Westminster Abbey. The Spencer family's conviction was that it was what Diana, Princess of Wales would have wanted. Wisely, all concerned eventually agreed to combine tradition and modernity. Radio stations had been heavily playing three Elton John songs following the news of Diana's death: Your Song, Don't Let The Sun Go Down On Me and Candle In The Wind. It was Candle that seemed most pertinent. Once Elton had received confirmation that he would perform at the ceremony from the Palace, he phoned Bernie, who was at home on his ranch at Santa Ynez, California.

Their initial thought was to write a new song in the vein of Candle In The Wind. In the end it seemed more sensible to keep the tune and see what new lyrics Bernie could come up with.

The original ode to that other blonde icon, Marilyn Monroe, written in 1973, had prescient words applicable to Diana. If sung in Westminster Abbey, its references to a devious Hollywood establishment would have been too close to the bitter truth: how she was made to change her name; how lonely she was; how she was still hounded by the press when she died; and how the price she paid was pain. Bernie had to strike out the sarcasm and poignancy and could only retrieve the lines: 'And it seemed to me you lived your life/Like a candle in the wind.'

If the song had been written by committee then it would have started, 'Goodbye Britain's rose...', or even 'Goodbye Wales' rose...'. There were objections raised to Bernie's choice of 'Goodbye England's rose...'. From Bernie's perspective, residing in California, England and Britain were pretty synonymous. And anyway, England somehow had more poetic grace within the rhythm of his words, and Bernie had always chosen the flow and sound of words over their meaning.

The wordsmith was feeling under intense pressure, but within 90 minutes of sitting down to write the song, he had the opening line. From then on, everything

Candle In The Wind 1997

flowed. Diana had died on Sunday, 31 August. Elton's invition to perform was made official on Thursday, 4 September, and the funeral was on Saturday, 6 September. For the songwriters who had created classics in minutes, it was not such an impossible task.

Bernie did not want to write a song that voiced his or Elton's personal viewpoint. He wanted to reflect the feelings of a nation in mourning. He made it hymn-like and, inevitably, sentimental. No-one wanted to hear about a gauche and gullible princess, they wanted an idealised version – which is what Bernie delivered with a mixture of aplomb and pedestrianism. 'You were the grace that places itself/Where lives were torn apart' exactly reflected what the Princess had aimed for and, in her most noble moments, achieved. He alluded, not for the first time, to William Blake's poem *Jerusalem*, with her footsteps on 'England's greenest hills'. There are 'the tears we cannot express' and 'the joy...[she]...brought through the years', which would not be out of place on a condolence card. But it all gelled. Bernie faxed the lyrics to Elton who rang him and told him the words were perfect.

At the service, after the Prime Minister Tony Blair had read the lesson from St. Paul, Elton went to his Yamaha piano to perform to in front of a televised audience of 2.5 billion. Facing him unseen from the cameras was a teleprompter. He needed the reassurance that he would sing the new words and not slip into the ones he had been familiar with for 24 years. Dressed elegantly in a Versace Nehru jacket he seemed composed, though his red, blinking eyes gave away his real emotional state. As he sang, it became too much for Princes Harry and William, who started sobbing. Such was the precise timing of the 64-minute service that Elton was given three minutes 45 seconds to perform his song. On its completion there was a sound which was unprecedented at such an occasion: applause rippled around the Abbey and filtered through from the crowds outside.

Elton went straight from the Abbey to The Town House Studios in Shepherds Bush where he had recorded The Big Picture album. The producer and arranger awaiting him was Sir George Martin. The same man who had turned down the job of producing Elton in 1969 because he wanted to do the arrangements, too. Over the years Martin had expressed a desire to someday work with Elton. They had already worked together on a Larry Adler album, The Glory Of Gershwin in 1994 and in 1995 Martin had arranged a number for the Made In England album. The original producer who had taken Martin's place, Gus Dudgeon, did not understand why Elton wanted to record the song when the live version from the Abbey was more powerful.

George Martin brought in a woodwind section, string quartet and his son Giles to co-produce. He suggested that Elton do the piano and voice live. On the second take Elton was pleased enough with what he had done for that to become the single. It is not surprising that Elton could not replicate the power of his Abbey performance. However the recorded version does resonate with the sorrow of the day. Martin was clearly keen to understate the music, allowing Elton's voice and piano to carry the emotional weight of the words. In the third verse the cellos tentatively underscore Elton and as the song builds, the rest of the strings and oboes join in for a repeat of the main lyrical theme of 'Goodbye England's rose...'. It reaches an intense finale as the strings sign off with the piano on a sustained note. Elton left the studio at 3.30 pm and received the master tape at home in Old Windsor before midnight.

The release of Elton's album The Big Picture and the single Something About The Way You Look Tonight had long been planned for September. Something would still be the single, but its release was put back a few days as it was now to be a double A-side with Candle In The Wind 1997. It was a canny marketing move that no-one could begrudge. The Diana, Princess of Wales Memorial Fund was to be the beneficiary of all profits.

The single went on sale in London, in the first minute of Saturday, 13 September. The first country to have copies had been France the day before. Demand everywhere in the world was unprecedented. After one day on sale in Britain it was at number one on the following day's chart. In America where it went on sale on 22 September, it sold over 3.4 million copies in its first week. The British Government waived Value Added Tax on the single (the first time since the Band Aid single Do They Know It's Christmas in 1985). Elton had hoped to raised £5-£10 million through sales of the record, but by the end of October he had raised £20 million. By year end he had outsold Bing Crosby's White Christmas and Candle in the Wind 1997 became the biggest selling single of all time with worldwide sales in excess of 33 million.

He will never perform the song live. "It's hers," he said. EU

Candle In The Wind 1997

TEN ESSENTIAL ELTON JOHN ALBUMS
1. Captain Fantastic And The Brown Dirt Cowboy.
2. Goodbye Yellow Brick Road
3. Elton John
4. Honky Chateau
5. Don't Shoot Me I'm Only The Piano Player
6. Tumbleweed Connection
7. Madman Across The Water
8. Sleeping With The Past
9. Blue Moves
10. Made In England

TEN ESSENTIAL ELTON JOHN ALIASES
1. Lord Choc Ice
2. Sir Humphrey Handbag
3. Sir Horace Pussy
4. Fanny Beaversnatchclip
5. Sharon Cavendish
6. William A. Bong
7. Commodore Orpington
8. Ebeneezer Moog
9. Bo Bo Latrine Latrine
10. Sir Brian Bigbum

Ten Essential Elton John Albums

BIBLIOGRAPHY

A Conversation with Elton John and Bernie Taupin
Paul Gambaccini, Flash, 1976

The Elton John Tapes: Elton John In Conversation '21 At 33'
Andy Peebles, BBC, 1981

Elton: The Definitive Biography
Philip Norman, Arrow, 1991

Two Rooms: Elton John and Bernie Taupin In Their Own Words
Boxtree, 1991

The Very Best Of Elton John
Wise Publications/Big Pig Music Limited, 1991

Elton John: A Visual Documentary
Nigel Goodall, Omnibus Press, 1993

The Many Lives Of Elton John
Susan Crimp and Patricia Burstein, Hale, 1993

The Complete Lyrics: Elton John and Bernie Taupin
Pavilion, 1994

Elton John 25 Years In The Charts
John Tobler, Hamlyn, 1995

Rocket Man: Elton John A-Z
Claude Bernardin and Tom Stanton, Praeger Publishers, 1996

Elton John's Flower Fantasies
Caroline Cass, Weidenfeld and Nicholson, 1997

Also available in this series

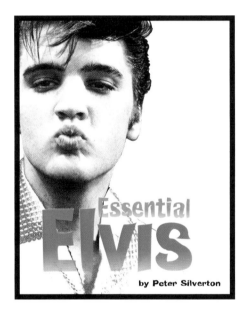

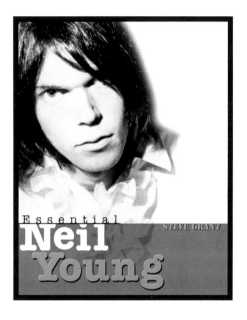

Essential Elvis
Peter Silverton
ISBN 0 233 99245 6

Essential Neil Young
Steve Grant
ISBN 0 233 99412 2

PICTURE CREDITS

Pictorial Press pages 8 (with Bernie Taupin), 12, 15, 19, 21, 34, 51,
    70 (with George Best), 80 (with Bernie Taupin), 102
Larry Ellis/Transworld Feature Syndicate page 22
David Refern/Redferns pages 24, 39
Terry O'Neill/Camera Press pages 26, 46, 67 (with Ringo Starr)
Ian Vaughan/Scope Features page 30
Bob Gruen/Pictorial Press page 44
Scope Features pages 55 (from *Tommy*), 62, 90, 113 (with Tim Rice)
Stephen F. Morley/Redferns page 56 (with John Lennon)
Richard Open/Camera Press page 60
Mayer/Pictorial Press page 68
Rex Features pages 77, 94, 109 (with Freddie Mercury)
Alan Davidson/Camera Press page 84 (with John Reid)
Camera Press page 86
Andy Earl/Retna Pictures page 92
Richard Young/Rex Features pages 98, 123 (with Diana)
Steve Granitz/Retna Pictures page 104
Piers Allardyce/SIN page 110
Edward Hirst/Rex Features page 119 (with David Furnish)

SOURCES

Various newspapers and magazines, notably: *NME*, *Melody Maker*, *Sounds*, *Rolling Stone*, *Mojo*, *Q*, *Vox*, *Billboard*, *Music Week*, *Record Collector*, the *Daily Mail*, the *Sun*, the *Daily Mirror*, the *Express*, *The Times*, *The Sunday Times*, the *Observer*, the *Independent*, the *Daily Telegraph*, the *Sunday Telegraph*, the *Evening Standard*.